SO YOU WANT TO BUILD A HOUSE

HOW TO BE YOUR OWN CONTRACTOR
J. RODNEY TAYLOR

BETTERWAY PUBLICATIONS, INC.
WHITE HALL, VIRGINIA

Published by Betterway Publications, Inc.
P.O. Box 219
Crozet, VA 22932
(804) 823-5661

Cover design by Rick Britton
Typography by Park Lane Associates

Library of Congress Cataloging-in-Publication Data

Taylor, J. Rodney (James Rodney)
    So you want to build a house : how to be your own contractor / J.
Rodney Taylor.
        p. cm.
    Includes index.
    ISBN 1-55870-185-0 (pbk.) : $14.95
    1. House construction--Amateurs' manuals. 2. Contractors-
-Amateurs' manuals. I. Title.
TH815.T38 1991
690'.837--dc20
                                                  90-21735
                                                   CIP

Printed in the United States of America
0 9 8 7 6 5 4 3 2

ACKNOWLEDGMENTS

There are so many people to whom I am indebted that it would be difficult to name them all. However, several individuals stand out, and I wish to direct public acknowledgment and appreciation to them. I would necessarily begin with those who have encouraged me to write this book. Those friends who have visited our home and who have offered encouragement both before and during the writing of this book deserve my utmost appreciation.

I wish to thank several individuals who were uniquely involved in the construction of my home and to whom I owe a real debt of gratitude. My thanks to Dan Cobb, the construction manager who assisted me every step of the way and gave me the education I needed to finish the job not only successfully but beautifully. To Dan, I owe a thank you from the bottom of my heart. To Debby Andrews and Don Williams of Alcor Mortgage for their invaluable assistance in researching and writing the information contained in the chapter on financing. And to Delmus Wilkinson, an inspector's inspector. He not only saw to it that our home was constructed according to code, he also performed his service in a polite and unassuming manner. I also owe

Delmus a thank you for assisting me in preparing and researching the portion of the book dealing with inspections and regulatory agencies. Thanks, Delmus, for taking your time to help.

To my mother, who died only eleven days prior to the occupancy of our new home, I owe special thanks. She knew I could build that house even during those times when I doubted it. She gave encouragement to me and became the sounding board I needed when times of frustration and discouragement arose. One of the rooms in our house is a constant reminder of her and her memory, for its plans and specifications were especially designed for "Miss Ruthie" in her elderly and more feeble years.

To my friend Gary Garland I wish to express sincere appreciation for his cooperation in allowing me to get the manuscript prepared with a minimum of difficulty. With friends like Gary, special projects are always less of a headache and easier to accomplish.

To my only remaining child at home — my daughter, Julie — who offered sensible suggestions on many decorating ideas as well as construction components, especially those relating to her bedroom. Her thoughtful suggestions and ability to soothe my nerves at times were greatly appreciated. I owe her a great big THANK YOU.

Finally, gratitude is expressed to my wife, Patty, who has had to listen, worry, speculate, anticipate, and experience loneliness during the time of construction as well as the period during which I have been writing this book. To her I owe a special thank you. While she may not have always understood why circumstances were as they were, she always encouraged. She shows with pride the results of my handiwork in the stained glass I fabricated for the house. She is pleased always to have visitors to whom she can "show off" her new home. To Patty, I express my lasting gratitude.

CONTENTS

INTRODUCTION

Ask almost any American couple about their dreams and aspirations and heading the list will be their desire for a house. This is why, in America, we call owning a house the "great American dream." While many couples would be happy to own any house, many families have their own ideas about the size, location, design, and amenities of their dream house. However, because of the escalating cost of residential construction, these families must settle for second best rather than their first priority. Cheer up! You *can* get what you want.

Let me begin by telling you a story. Once upon a time there were a man and a woman who loved each other very much. While still in college, they decided to be married. For thirty years they struggled with life, enjoying each other's company, enjoying the pleasurable times with their children, and putting as much into life as possible. Through the years they had occupied rental apartments and houses they had purchased in each of the towns and cities in which they lived. But they had never been able to build that "dream house" that they had so long desired. Finally, they came to a momentous decision.

After having invested in a subdivision lot in an upscale residential neighborhood, they decided to build their dream house. But the only way they could afford it would be to build it themselves. PROBLEM! She was a school teacher with no credentials in construction and no building skill to do the job herself; he was an educator and consultant with only modest knowledge of construction and absolutely no skill in driving nails, laying brick, or calculating roof chords. But they were determined not to let that deter them. So they put the wheels in motion.

Today, our couple has that dream house, a house with more space than they ever dreamed that they might be able to afford—3,700 square feet of living space. In a home which includes marble floors and marble window sills, parquet floors, the highest quality carpeting and flooring, stained glass, and other value-enhancing amenities, the home was constructed for approximately $29 per square foot or 25 to 35% less than it would have cost for contractor construction. And it was made possible through the process of self-contracting.

That is what this book is all about — self-contracting. In this book you will learn how to work with a designer to get the kind of look you want in your home. You will learn the "buzzwords" to use in obtaining a construction loan and building materials and in dealing with subcontractors. You will learn how to enlist subcontractors, how to negotiate on materials prices, scheduling, and other important considerations to be made in the process. This is a how-to book to help you understand the process and to offer step-by-step information on self-contracting.

This book is drawn from my own experience. It is not based on theory. It is written primarily upon the recommendation of several of my friends who wish to construct new homes but who do not have the requisite knowledge or experience to do so themselves. They have asked that I put in writing the benefits of my experience and thus help others, who, like themselves, wish to realize their dream. To them and to my wife who "endured" the experience, I dedicate this book.

1

THE CONSTRUCTION PROCESS
How to Begin

Consider this scenario. A couple has purchased a residential lot with a dream of owning a home there for some time. They have looked at plans, talked with builders, attended more "Parades of Homes" than they ever thought necessary, and reconsidered their personal and family priorities on many nights before the blazing fireplace just to make sure that a new home was really what they wanted more than anything else. Needless to say, all the time spent resulted in disappointment, because the plans they studied didn't really match their needs at the moment, the builders with whom they talked quoted prices that were completely out of reach, "Parade" homes were always the ideal with amenities and building materials they would never be able to afford.

To top off all these frustrations, on those nights when they sat before the fire reconsidering their priorities, those priorities seemed to change. At one time they felt the need for a large house with several bedrooms and baths. At another time, fewer bedrooms and baths will serve the family but closet space is a greater need. At still another time, storage space, including large storage areas, becomes a high priority. And the fundamental determining factor underlying all

of these elements is the concern for funding the project. How will the family be able to pay for it? As much as they would like to have this beautiful home, how is it possible, especially when money is such a major consideration?

In the construction of any home, the cost of that construction is always a factor to be considered. The final price of a home is the combined total of the cost of the lot on which the house will be built, the materials to be used in the home itself, labor costs to construct the home, and miscellaneous costs incurred through regulatory or other means. These last costs often are not controllable. Through self-contracting, not only will significant dollar savings be realized in the construction process itself, but assurances of payment and other factors can be controlled, thus reducing the overall expense in constructing the house.

So although the *cost* of the house is a major factor, you must be aware that the cost *can* be controlled. By controlling those elements of the construction process that can be controlled, the expense to you, the buyer/builder, is much less, and the home often becomes affordable when otherwise it might not have been.

This chapter is designed to help you know when and how to start your own home through self-contracting. It will introduce you to a step-by-step process beginning with the design phase and extending through the construction phase to that important day when you occupy your new home. Furthermore, this chapter introduces each of the chapters that follow and offers an understanding of and advice and counsel upon attitudes, abilities, and personal characteristics required to bring a residential construction project to a successful conclusion.

GETTING STARTED

Probably the most difficult aspect of any task is knowing how to begin. When you decide to build your own home, there are specific steps required to make the beginning a smooth one. No step in the process, however trivial it may appear, should be skipped. Each step is designed to bring you closer to getting the kind of house you want without having to make changes of such magnitude that you end up with a house with which you might be dissatisfied.

Location

Every city and town in America has living areas that are more desirable than others. As you consider building your dream house, make a special effort to determine precisely where you would like that house to be located. Talk with any real estate agent, and that person will tell you that the most important factor in real estate is *location, location, location!* If you ever expect to sell your home in the future—and most people do—location is the primary factor in its salability.

The first step in seeking a homesite is *research.* Remember, you will probably be putting the greatest amount of your personal resources into your home. Therefore, finding the right homesite is primary to making sure that the home will retain its value over time.

One caveat is necessary at this point; namely, that areas of desirable living today may not be areas of desirable living twenty years from now. However, this first step in the process of locating a desirable homesite will minimize the likelihood of a poor future location. But you are probably asking: How and what kind of research is necessary to achieve this goal?

Begin the process by reviewing the development of the city or county in which you plan to build. I suggest that you review data for a period covering the immediate past ten to fifteen years. Information can be obtained from the local planning boards or planning councils, whichever are operative in your state. Or you may visit the permit office of the governmental entity (city, county, or township) you are reviewing. I suggest that you review data from both the city and county permit offices.

In the case of counties or townships with planning boards or councils, the data typically found there will generally involve both city and county development. Talk with staff members who have been with these agencies for an extended period of time—more than two or three years—and ask them about the areas of most rapid development. For sales data on homes, check with a local residential appraiser to ascertain the possible existence of a monthly home sales database, which will provide the pertinent information regarding home sales, locations, and prices. If such a database does not exist, inquire of the appraiser concerning some of the factors listed below. The factors you should look for in making your determination include:

1. Geographical sectors in which the greatest development has occurred.

2. Location and build-out of subdivisions or developments in the value range anticipated for your home.

3. Existence of zoning ordinances in the county, municipality, or township.

4. Existence of constraining factors that might lower values, such as commercial land too

close to residential property, nearby airports or other transportation hubs, or a high turnover rate in home sales.

5. Prices of lots in planned developments or raw land not included in planned developments. ("Planned developments" in this instance means platted subdivisions.)

6. Availability of utilities such as sewer services, water, natural gas, and cable TV. Take special note if these services are underground, for underground utilities add both value and salability to your home.

After data from these interviews and reviews have been gathered, it is advisable to reduce your areas of interest to two or three specific geographical areas. It is now time for you to take a leisurely Sunday afternoon drive in those sectors of the city or county you are interested in to seek out lots for sale or raw land available in unplatted subdivisions. Look for signs by real estate firms or by owners. Be sure to have with you a pencil or pen and several copies of the Properties of Interest form (see Appendix). Record information on the lots that appeal to you. When you find a piece of property that interests you, make a note of the real estate company, the name of the listing agent, the phone number of the real estate company, and the after hours number for the listing agent. Also provide a brief notated description of the property and its location. Location may be described as the "north side of Oak Street in the 3200 block." Other notations might include "trees," "sloping lot," approximate dimensions, and brief descriptions of adjoining homes.

The Properties of Interest form can serve you well also for property being sold by owners. The same procedures used with property being marketed by real estate firms apply to property for sale by owners. The only difference is that you will be making a note of the owner's name and telephone number rather than that of a real estate agent. Be sure to include all data, such as a brief description of the property and other identifiable data.

Negotiation

After you have identified several parcels of property of interest, rank the properties in order of your level of interest. If information is available on the sale of lots in a particular area, investigate those sales, carefully noting the size of the lots sold, whether or not the lot is located on a corner, and the price of each lot. Information on these sales is available through local database services, the county courthouse, the local Board of Realtors, or a real estate appraiser. If you are not sure whether the area has a local, private sector home sales database service, ask a real estate appraiser. If such services are available, the real estate appraiser will know. Remember, when you are researching your comparable sales, *do not compare house sales with lot sales.* A form entitled Comparable Sales is provided in the Appendix for your convenience in recording the sales data. Compare these data with the lot or lots you are interested in to arrive at a fair price for each. After determining a fair price, firmly establish the highest price you will pay for the property and place that figure on the Properties of Interest form.

My suggestion is always to begin the negotiation process by making an offer 20 to 25% below the market value, which you have established by reviewing comparable sales. In certain markets where lot sales may be slow, you may wish to begin negotiation at an even lower level.

Comparable sales are the commonly-used means to determine a fair price on any piece of property. As mentioned above, comparable sales can be found in a local home sales database (if available), at the local office of the Recorder of Deeds, or with the local Board of Realtors. Keep in mind, however, that the Board of Realtors generally maintains records only of those sales handled by their members. The more complete records are maintained at the Deed Recorder's office located in your county courthouse or county seat town. Another alternative would be to contact a real estate appraiser and ask for his or her input into the comparable sales review.

You may have to promise the appraiser to use his services at the time of purchase, but such a compromise might well be worth it, since you will get accurate and useful comparable sales data.

With comparable sales data in hand, you have a good starting point and room for negotiation. Remember, there is a point beyond which you will *not* negotiate. That point is the price you have established as the highest price you are willing to pay. By performing the comparable sales study, you have determined the level at which you may obtain a bargain price for a residential lot. Probably my most sound advice at this point is: *Do not become emotionally involved with any piece of property*. When a person becomes emotionally involved in real estate, genuine negotiation is generally compromised or forfeited, the price rises, and the buyer pays a premium for property that might have been purchased at a more reasonable price or even at a bargain.

Negotiate on each parcel of property based on the information obtained and the highest price you are willing to pay. Start with the lot in which you are *most* interested and continue negotiations on that lot until either the seller meets your terms or you determine that further negotiation is useless. If you are unable to reach an agreement, then proceed to the next piece of property on your list. Repeat the process until you have obtained a lot that meets your needs. With luck, the process will have worked well enough for you to have purchased a lot at less than regular market value.

WHERE FROM HERE?!

Now that you have obtained a site on which to construct your home, the real fun begins. This section is a step-by-step overview of the entire process, beginning with the design phase and extending through the construction phase to occupation. Typically, the steps that follow outline the chapters in the remainder of this book and

provide introduction thereto. So read these sections carefully; they will provide an excellent introduction to the chapters that follow.

Design

A major step in the process of construction, whether by a contractor or by the self-contractor, is the design of the home to be built. It is important to get the "look" that you desire with as much space as you can afford. Keep in mind that by self-contracting you probably can construct up to 30% more space for the same dollars than you would have spent by using a licensed residential contractor.

Many variables in the design process go into determining the final price of the house. Thus the key to getting a good start on a home is its design. The selection of and cooperation with the designer is of utmost importance. The chapter on design will outline the procedure for selecting and working with the designer. In that chapter, we will discuss the process of selecting a designer and the qualifications sought in a designer. The chapter will also include the elements that should be included in a contract with a designer, a timeline for completion of the design work, cost factors, design control, final design, and implementation of the design. Other factors to be discussed include the level of involvement of the designer in the construction phase, his authority during construction, his consultation services at times when problems arise during construction, and his payment schedule.

Terminology

Knowing and understanding the "buzzwords" used in the construction industry will pay off more than any other knowledge. A working knowledge of words and phrases used in construction will make it possible for you to convince both a mortgage company and a local building inspector's office that you actually know what you are doing. This is important because the mortgage company considering a construction loan will want to know whether you can actually do what you say you can do. Furthermore, the building inspector's office, whose responsibility it is to issue the building permits, also wants to make sure that a construction permit is not being issued to a project that might be halted or left unfinished due to the inability of the contractor to complete the work. And this attitude exists regardless of the presence of state or county legislation allowing for self-contracting.

Chapter 3, therefore, provides those buzzwords, along with an explanation of their meanings and their relative importance to the process. An understanding of these terms will endear the self-contractor both to the prospective mortgage company considering the construction loan and to the subcontractors and the regulatory inspectors. A working knowledge of the terminology generates and conveys self-confidence and a grasp of the entire process.

Financing

Before actual construction is initiated, adequate funds must be available to complete the job. Therefore, financing becomes one of the pivotal problems with self-contracting, for the source you go to for financing, either construction or permanent, must be convinced that financing your self-contracted home presents no more risk to the lender than would the same home constructed by a licensed contractor.

Few families have the necessary capital in savings to accomplish the task of house construction, so they must rely on mortgage bankers to provide the funds. As you pursue funds for construction, you need to be informed about the process of seeking construction and permanent financing. Furthermore, the importance of obtaining both types of financing simultaneously cannot be overstated.

There are a number of types of financing available, and they must be evaluated carefully. The chapter on financing explains the various types of financing available and offers an evaluation of each; describes in detail the purposes, forms, and conditions of both construction and permanent financing; and offers advice on seeking and finding the most advantageous and attractive financing package.

In conjunction with financing is the importance of getting accurate and complete pre-construction appraisals and insurance. The pre-construction appraisal will assist the self-contractor and the mortgage company in ascertaining, with a reasonable degree of certainty, the amount for which the construction loan should be issued and certified.

From the perspective of insurance, it is possible to buy an insurance package including provisions covering the construction phase. The package then rolls over into a common homeowner's policy, requiring no additional prepaid premiums or deposits. Thus, because they are a part of the process, pre-construction appraisals and insurance will be discussed as a part of this chapter.

Inspectors

No residential construction anywhere in the United States is carried out without the approval of certain regulatory agencies. These agencies may be a part of a state, township, county, or municipal government. But whatever type of governmental subdivision they belong to, these regulatory agencies hold powerful influence over the final outcome of the home. In most cases, the regulations (state or local) governing the building inspections departments of some of these governmental subdivisions provide for a person to serve as his or her own contractor in the case of residential construction. However, it is extremely important to understand the operations of these departments, the roles they play, and how to get along with them with minimal difficulty.

While oftentimes inspectors appear to be unreasonable in their demands, they actually perform an important function—making sure that construction is structurally sound and is designed and constructed according to specifications providing the greatest margin of safety. So this chapter will provide an overview of the types of inspections that might be required—both preconstruction and during construction. Further, we will discuss what might be expected from these inspections, how to prepare for such inspections, and important tips on how to avoid conflict with the inspectors.

Building Materials

Probably the most important and financially draining element to be included in your house is the construction materials. The quality of the building materials will, in many ways, determine the quality of the home you build. Furthermore, the materials used in your home can determine the potential life of the structure, its strength, and its ability to withstand natural disaster.

While building materials are likely the most critical element in your house construction, they are also a major source of expenditure. And while significant amounts of money will be spent on building materials, it is not necessary for the self-contractor to pay a premium price for such materials.

In the chapter on building materials, a strategy for negotiating prices and terms with suppliers of building materials will be outlined. Also discussed are the establishment of credit accounts, COD orders, the advantages and disadvantages of certain payment schedules (e.g., COD vs. net or discount terms), and what might be expected, in terms of negotiating strategy, from the various types of suppliers.

Subcontractors

Almost everyone who talks to me about self-contracting wants to know how to find subcontractors, sometimes called "subs." And there certainly is a process that can be used both to find subcontractors and to investigate the quality of their work. This chapter will offer the secret to this part of the plan. The chapter will outline at least three ways in which subcontractors can be identified, contacted, enlisted, and investigated or evaluated.

After identifying and reviewing the work of the subcontractors to be contacted for the specific type of work to be completed—and remember, there will be more than one subcontractor identified for each element of the project—then negotiation regarding cost and time elements can be initiated. The art of negotiation is nowhere better exercised than in dealing with subcontractors. They are a sub-culture all to themselves, and it is essential that you understand that subculture, the nature of its operations, and the economic constraints under which it functions. There is considerable room for negotiation on almost every element in the construction plan, and Chapter 7 will provide a step-by-step plan for negotiating with subcontractors.

Construction Management

The difference between this book and other books written on the subject is that you can function as your own contractor and not have to have extensive experience in or knowledge of construction techniques and processes. In fact, you may not be able to saw a piece of lumber straight, but you certainly can function as your own contractor. The secret is basically twofold: (1) Putting in the *time* required and (2) enlisting an expert to assist you. It is best, therefore, to negotiate and contract with a licensed contractor or someone both highly skilled and broadly experienced in construction, preferably a person with a reputation for honesty and quality, who can serve as a construction manager.

In today's market, there are those persons who are taking the time to learn the construction trade, sitting for the state or other required licensing examinations, and putting themselves into business as "building consultants." They generally advertise themselves as managers of construction projects. Therefore, in proceeding with self-contracting, you must be careful to investigate thoroughly those who advertise themselves as construction managers. Chapter 8 deals with the job of the construction manager, what should be included in the contract, relative costs for such services, and some of the ways in which the construction manager can be of assistance during the construction phase.

Amenities

Amenities are those items that typically make the cost of the home rise or fall. And, believe it or not, the cost of a home is probably most controlled by the amenities included. Marble floors or counter tops vs. carpeted floors and laminated counter tops, parquet vs. finished wood, paint finish cabinetry vs. stain finished cabinetry, carpeting vs. wood floors, porcelain, statuary, swimming pools, saunas, tennis courts — all such amenities, and these are only a few, typically control the cost of the home. If these costs are controlled, then the overall cost of the home can be controlled. Chapter 9 discusses amenities, the relative additional cost of selected amenities, how to control the costs of some of these amenities, and the contribution they make to both the expense and the look of the home.

Pitfalls

As with any project of value you might become involved in, self-contracting will have its share of pitfalls. To say that a house can be self-contracted without frustration, difficulty, problems, or "headaches" would be a gross misstatement. Even the most experienced licensed contractor will tell you that construction is, at its best, a fun and satisfying experience but, at its worst, an absolute nightmare. And if such is the case with the licensed or experienced contractor, how can it be less for the self-contractor?

Every self-contractor can expect the same problems that befall a licensed contractor, who is in the business to make money. And, in fact, some of the problems will be magnified by the fact that you are building only one house, while the licensed contractor has the potential for multiple construction opportunities. Chapter 10 describes some of the pitfalls and woes that beset the self-contractor and how to deal with them. This chapter also provides some mental health counseling to help the future homeowner maintain the proper attitude for functioning as a self-contractor.

Moving Day

Moving day has finally arrived! The dream suddenly comes into focus. All of the woes and problems, all of the frustrations and negotiations, all of the pains and difficulty fade into obscurity on the day you move into the home that you have so methodically, meticulously, and painstakingly planned and constructed. The joy of that day is described, along with what might be expected during the first year you occupy the house. Chapter 11 deals with the problems that might be encountered after moving day and specific actions to take to deal appropriately with such problems.

THE BEST ADVICE

I would be remiss if I did not share several important thoughts about self-contracting early in this book. These considerations can make or break the success of your self-contracting project and can result in frustrations more severe than you are able to bear if they are not understood and dealt with early in the process. Essentially, they are the mental health foundation stones upon which the project will proceed. *And they must be considered* because the success of your project will, in large measure, be determined by these three crucial factors.

Attitudes

The first of these factors is *attitude*. Your attitude toward the plan, the project, and the process of self-contracting will often determine how well you handle the problems of the project, how readily you are able to determine solutions to these problems, and how well you work with the other people involved in your project.

While this book is not intended to be a volume for the amateur psychologist, it is necessary that the potential self-contractor conduct some self-evaluation prior to undertaking a task as economically far-reaching as building his own home. In so doing, the following attitudes must be present.

The first attitude is a willingness to accept the challenge, a willingness to take the risk. By the time you have completed reading and understanding this book, you will be aware of all that is involved in the complicated process of constructing your own home. And in order for that project to be completed successfully, you must be willing to accept the challenge, along with all the sacrifices that will be required. The challenge will include preparation required, time to be invested, continuing absences from family at times, continual review of plans and specifications, constantly being on the telephone ordering supplies or contacting subcontractors, to name only a few.

While it is not necessary for you to be at the job site all day every day, your presence there is needed periodically if the job is to progress smoothly. You must be willing to put in that required time, and your family must also be willing to give you up for the time you need to be on the job. Remind your family of the enjoyment they will experience as a result of the time you spend now on your new home. And remind them also that the inconvenience is only temporary.

The second attitude is persistence. It is often necessary to refuse to take no for an answer. You must be ready, willing, and able to take a persistent stand upon certain matters as they arise. For example, if your framing contractor indicates that a wall should be moved from the planned location to another location, be prepared to stand firm in maintaining the original location, if that location was determined for a specific reason. If not, be flexible enough to listen and then make a determination based on logic and reason. However, no matter what the case, maintain a persistent attitude throughout the process.

In the case of regulatory matters, persistence is also required. If an inspector comes, inspects the house, and requires an action you know to be in violation of or not required by code, be persistent yet sensitive enough to make your voice heard. Most inspectors will listen and agree if the demand is not a matter of law. Thus, be persistent and stand your ground when you know you are right.

A third attitude can best be described as assertiveness/aggressiveness. If you are a person who tends to be a pushover for someone else, you probably will not be successful in supervising and contracting your own home. The self-contractor will be a person who is both assertive, that is, willing to let his voice be heard, and aggressive. Aggressiveness, in this case, means willing to step out on limbs, if necessary, to achieve certain goals. For example, if, in searching for building products, you find that one company offers a higher price on shingles but a lower price on roofing felt than another company, be aggressive enough to ask the manager of the former company to lower his price on the shingles to that of the second company so that you can purchase both the shingles and the roofing felt from him. In most cases, he will lower his price to get the business. But the self-contractor cannot be so intimidated by the supplier that he is unwilling to *ask* for the lower price. You will be surprised at the times that suppliers or subcontractors will lower their prices just to get the business.

Assertiveness means that you express yourself in an honest way, making your true feelings known, but not hurting others in the process. It means that you do not allow others to walk all over you and make you change your mind when you know that your own ideas are best. In other words, be willing to stand your ground but in a way that will gain or maintain the respect of others.

Abilities

Another important factor to be considered when self-contracting is the ability to do the job properly. Being a self-contractor does not require a college education; it does not require an intricate and detailed knowledge of building procedures; it does not require the innate ability to construct. It does require, however, such abilities as communication, arbitration/negotiation, and management.

A person who lacks the ability to communicate will have a difficult time functioning as a self-contractor. Whether you are dealing with a subcontractor, your construction manager, a supplier, or an inspector, it is absolutely essential that you be able to communicate clearly and concisely. Communication here means to convey a clear meaning of what you are trying to say without outside influences like shouting, cursing, or over-reactive gestures. In most cases, firmness, combined with fact, will accomplish your goal. For example, suppose you are facing a critical inspection. When the inspector arrives, he tells you that you will have to replace the entire front door because the glass is not tempered according to code. If you have done your homework, you will know that the code does not require that the entire door be replaced, but only the glass. And it may not even be necessary to replace the glass, depending upon the type of glass installed. Thus armed with the facts and a resolve not to be forced to do something not required, be firm with the inspector, citing the code and asking him politely to review the code to make sure that he is right. Such an effort will buy time, will help the inspector become better acquainted with the code he is asked to enforce,

and will ultimately result in your position being supported. An ancillary result will be a greater respect for you on the part of the inspector out of recognition of your knowledge of what's required. So communication becomes an important ability, which will often be put to use during the course of the construction.

A second ability is that of arbitration-negotiation. This ability is especially useful when dealing with subcontractors and materials suppliers. More will be said about negotiations in Chapter 6. Suffice it to say here that you should hone your skills in negotiation to make the system work for you as you proceed through the construction process.

A third ability is that of management. A person with the ability to see beyond the moment will be more successful at the construction process than the person who lacks managerial ability. A manager is one who sees the "big picture," the whole job as well as the pieces that make up the whole. He has the ability to break the job down into small increments, managing each increment as it is presented. He has the ability to deal with the problems that arise with detachment, objectivity, and resolve.

The manager knows how to deal with the time factor. Time is always a factor the self-contractor must reckon with. It may be the time factor in the construction period caused by some outside force uncontrolled or uncontrollable by the self-contractor; it may be time considerations based on weather conditions or projected weather conditions; it may be time influenced by anticipated price changes in materials or labor. But whatever the reason, time often becomes a critical factor. The self-contractor with good managerial ability can chart the time factor as construction progresses, knowing when to call certain subcontractors, when to order specific materials, when to call for inspections, etc.

Good management ability also calls for good interpersonal relationships. How easy do you think it will be to get the framer to work steadily on your house if you are there badgering him and his crew about being too slow? Or how cooperative do you think the inspector will be if you follow him around during the inspection and tell him that he is being too picky about certain requirements? One of the most useful tools in the bag of any individual who deals with others is the ability to manage people without their feeling manipulated or violated. The good manager knows how to deal with people as persons. And that ability will go a long way toward easing any problems that might arise on the job site.

Personal Characteristics

A final factor to be considered is that of personal characteristics. Personal characteristics are those elements that are unseen but so very important. While time and space do not permit a thorough examination of all the characteristics required by the self-contractor, a few will be mentioned and discussed.

The first of these characteristics is enthusiasm or motivation. If you are not genuinely enthusiastic about the prospects of building your own home or if your motivation is ill-founded, you are advised not to take on this task. But if you can visualize the challenge, anticipate the joys, and look forward with enthusiasm to the project itself, then you are well on your way to an enjoyable and rewarding experience.

Other characteristics essential to the process include:

❏ Self-confidence: You must be confident that you are not taking on a project that will defeat you. Confidence, tempered with a willingness to learn, will go a long way toward bringing success to the project. Furthermore, it is this confidence in yourself that will motivate others to have confidence in you.

❏ Integrity: Be a person of your word. Be firm but honest in all your dealings. If you make a mistake in judgment, admit it and proceed. Project to those you work with a sense of integrity

and ethical behavior. You will be surprised how others will react to you in the same manner.

❏ Decisiveness: One of the best characteristics you can possess is decisiveness. Do not be wishy-washy. Sometimes it is better to be decisively wrong than to change your mind constantly. In the case of a wrong decision, ninety-nine times out of a hundred, the wrong can be righted. But a wishy-washy approach causes others to lose confidence in you.

❏ Cooperation: If you have ever heard the phrase, "you can attract more flies with honey than with vinegar," you understand the importance of a cooperative spirit. By making every effort to be cooperative, you can often reduce the frustration of the project by eliminating stressful situations. Cooperation with subcontractors and inspectors is especially helpful in reducing your stress level.

❏ Flexibility: You are advised to be firm but flexible. Have your way understood but be willing to allow for unforeseen circumstances which may arise. Flexibility will also help reduce your stress level as you proceed with the job.

❏ Knowledge: While it is certainly not necessary that you be familiar with all the codes, laws, and regulations that might impinge on your construction project, it is important to be informed about these codes, laws, and regulations, where to find them, and how to use them to your advantage. Being informed about the ways subcontractors bid jobs, being knowledgeable about the units in which building materials are sold, having at least a cursory knowledge of reading blueprints, being able to visualize how an element will look when finished—these are but a few of the ways in which being informed will be an asset to you as a self-contractor.

MEETING THE CHALLENGE

You are now ready to begin the challenging journey toward realizing your dream house.

And you will realize that dream for considerably less money than you ever thought possible. The reason: YOU WILL BE THE BUILDER.

This first chapter has been designed to help you prepare yourself for what can be a rewarding experience. By carefully reading the chapter and heeding its admonitions you will be adequately prepared to meet this challenge successfully. The chapters that follow will outline, in detail, the "how" of getting the job done and getting it done well. The rewards, both in terms of personal accomplishment and money saved, will be immeasurable.

2

WORKING WITH A DESIGNER
Getting That Look

"How in the world could he put a glass-walled bathroom on the front of that house?" "Gee, I never saw a bedroom off the foyer before." "What! A bathroom with the toilet facing a front window?" These are actual quotations which have been heard regarding the designs of homes that were a part of a Parade of Homes. They point out the fact that there are about as many designs as there are people, and a design appreciated by one person may not be appreciated by another. So the natural conclusion is that house design is fundamental to all that follows in the process of house construction.

The key to getting a good start on a home is its design. From the selection of the designer to the final design result, the relationship between the designer and the self-contractor is one of utmost importance. In this chapter, the procedure for working with the designer will be outlined. Also discussed are such topics as selecting the designer, qualifications sought in a designer, expectations from the designer, contractual terms, and other critical issues the self-contractor must be aware of with regard to the design and the designer.

SELECTING A DESIGNER

One of the more frustrating exercises in self-contracting is the selection of the person to design the house. As the self-contractor, you are generally well aware of what you want in a house; all you need is someone who can put that concept on paper in a way that is both physically sound and aesthetically appealing. So the natural question to arise at this point is: What should I look for in a home designer?

AVOID NEGATIVE CHARACTERISTICS

Home designers come in every shape, size, and capability imaginable. The real key to selecting a designer is to find one you can work with effectively, efficiently, and with a minimum of difficulty. The self-contractor should be careful to avoid designers with certain characteristics. These characteristics include the following:

A Defensive Attitude

When initial contact with a designer is made, be sure to request samples of the work the designer has completed and, preferably, has carried through construction. If there are elements of the design that do not please you, make the designer aware of your feelings and the reasons for them. The response of the designer will give the self-contractor a cue as to the attitude of the designer with regard to any defensive nature. If the designer is overly defensive, proceed to another choice. Be careful, however, not to confuse defensiveness with genuine reason and logic for a specific design.

The major reason you should avoid the defensive designer is that, in all likelihood, the final result will be the designer's plan rather than that of the self-contractor. The designer with a defensive nature tends to protect his designs much as an artist would protect his artwork. But in this case, the art involves a house you might live with for the next ten to thirty years. The home should have the appearance and plan *you* like, not what appeals to the designer's tastes. Of course, the appearance and plan you wish to implement must be sound physically. It is the designer's responsibility to see that the desired plan can, in fact, be engineered soundly.

An Arrogant Attitude

Arrogance on the part of the designer will almost always result in the designer having his or her way. The attitude conveyed is that the designer knows more than the self-contractor, and he should be the person to make the final determination as to the floor plan and the elevation design. This "know-it-all" attitude will almost always carry over into the construction phase and will make it difficult, at best, for the self-contractor to maintain a strong management or supervisory role during the construction phase. The designer will tend to take over, leaving the self-contractor defenseless in dealing with the subcontractors and materials suppliers.

The 2-3 designer

This designer is characterized by mass produc-tion. He typically has two, three, or more floor plans, which he alternates from one client to another with the elevations being the only noticeable differences. Elevations are scale drawings or designs of the front, back, and side views of a house. Understand that the key here is not the specific number of floor plans available but that the number of floor plans is limited. When you visit the designer's office, be careful to scrutinize closely the work that is displayed to avoid the 2-3 floor plan scheme. Ask for as many different floor plans and elevations as the designer will show. And study them carefully. Do not review them in haste. Be willing to ask the designer if you may take two or three plans home with you for study. If he will not permit several sets of plans to be studied, that may be an indication of potential trouble.

SEEK POSITIVE CHARACTERISTICS

Now that you know what to avoid in selecting a designer, what are some of the positive characteristics the self-contractor should seek in a designer? Remember that the design is fundamental to all that will follow. If the design is faulty, then the structure could very well be faulty. If the elevation is not appealing, then the homeowner/self-contractor will be unhappy yet unable to make alterations without unnecessary expense.

When searching for that "right" person to design your home, look for some of the following characteristics.

A Team Player

The designer should have a pleasing, easygoing personality; he should be a team player. It is easy to work with the person with a pleasing personality. Even when differences of opinion occur, the easygoing designer does not become overly excited, defensive, or close-minded. If the design is sound, he will say so but explain his reluctance. If, however, the self-contractor desires to retain the design, the designer capitulates to the wishes of the homeowner. If the design is not sound from the standpoint of physics and engineering, then the designer explains the problems caused by the element and makes reasonable alternative suggestions to design the element as closely as possible to the wishes of the homeowner, but with sound engineering techniques applied.

The designer who exhibits this characteristic makes the design process a smooth and enjoyable experience. Moreover, the homeowner gets the idea that the design is his and his alone, not that of the designer. In such a case, the designer becomes a facilitator who is only interested in providing a plan both he and the homeowner can be equally proud of.

This characteristic is probably best observed through a series of meetings with the prospective designer. During these meetings, make sure you explore a variety of ideas, ascertain his attitude toward such ideas, and observe his personal and professional reactions. The observant homeowner will recognize quite quickly the designer who wants to be a team player.

Available and Accessible

Have you ever had a problem with your home air conditioning system and made a call to an air conditioning repair service only to find that the repair service was closed and the repairman unavailable or inaccessible? And after numerous attempts to make contact with the repairman, you simply gave up trying. If you think such a situation is unacceptable, try building a house using a designer who is neither available nor accessible, especially at times when he may be needed most.

The availability/accessibility factor is not limited to the design phase only. It applies to all phases of the process. For example, during construction, a design flaw might be discovered by the framing crew. The designer must be available to come to the site, review the plans, take note of the flaw, and recommend a solution. If the designer is neither available nor accessible, it will be necessary for the framing crew to lose a day's work or even more waiting for the designer to inspect the situation and make corrections.

Availability means that the designer can make appointments regarding your home plan without excessive alterations to either his or your schedule. It means further that he can meet you in your home or at his office, whichever location is most convenient to you. He is available for consultation at hours other than regular office hours and can be counted on to meet his appointments promptly. During construction, he is available, within a reasonable length of time, to deal with an emergency.

Accessibility means that your designer can be reached by phone during office hours or at least can be expected to return your phone calls promptly upon his return to the office. If the situation arises in which you must see the designer during office hours, he is accessible within a reasonable length of time.

These characteristics are best determined not by asking the designer himself but rather by asking others who have used the services of the designer in question. Ask him for references of contractors or other homeowners with whom he has worked in the recent past. Obtain names and telephone numbers and the approximate dates during which the designer worked with the contractor or homeowner. Place calls to the homeowners first, simply because they would have been functioning in the same or a similar capacity to your present situation. Follow the calls to homeowners with calls to the contractors. Key questions might include:

❑ How often was it necessary for you to meet with Mr. Jones prior to the completion of the plan?

❑ Did Mr. Jones often have conflicts with his schedule?

❑ Did Mr. Jones readily make appointments after regular office hours?

❑ Did Mr. Jones agree to a limited number of sketches before the final drawings or did he readily make changes without regard for the number of sketches being requested?

❑ Did Mr. Jones always meet with you in his office or did he agree to meet you in your home?

❑ Did Mr. Jones limit the amount of time he spent with you at each session or did he prefer to stay until the problems were resolved?

❑ Did Mr. Jones promptly return your phone calls during the design period?

❑ Were you generally pleased with the amount of time spent on each element of the plan?

❑ Did Mr. Jones take full responsibility for the design or did he transfer that responsibility to another person within the firm? Were you pleased with the results?

Answers to these questions will provide the homeowner/self-contractor with a basis on which to determine the relative availability/accessibility of the prospective designer. If the answers to these questions are unsatisfactory, proceed to the next prospect and repeat the process. Continue repeating the process until you are satisfied that the designer can meet your criteria for selection.

Professional Capability

Professional capability is probably the most important factor to be considered. If the prospective designer does not have the credentials or the basic mental and physical capacity to perform, he cannot be expected to do a satisfactory job. In considering professional capability, you are probably asking yourself, "What do I know that makes me an expert in evaluating the work of a designer?" That's an excellent question! And I am about to give you the answer.

First, look for a designer who is practical in his approach to house plans. There are many designers to choose from, and it is your responsibility to find the right one. To select a person who takes a position of impracticality is unwise. The prospective designer should be able to listen to the desires of the homeowner and put those desires into a reasonable and workable plan. So the designer should be practical in his approach to the plan.

The designer should also be practical in his approach to the site. He should not try to plan for a structure that is incompatible with the residential area in which the home is to be located. He should take into account the topography of the site, the vegetation located on the site, and the covenant restrictions, if any exist. (See Chapter 3 for a definition of covenants.)

Second, the designer should be creative and imaginative. While the homeowner may have an idea of what he would like to have included in the home, often he does not know how he would like to have it arranged. The designer should be able to take the basic ideas of the homeowner and draw them into a preliminary sketch to give the homeowner a general plan.

The designer should be able to think of creative ways to include important elements without the attendant high costs that often accompany them. He should find imaginative and alternative approaches to floor plans, layout, traffic patterns, and elevation designs that will express the lifestyle, character, and social status of the homeowner for whom the design is being prepared. He should be familiar with the various styles of homes—from contemporary and modern to the more traditional and neoclassic.

Creativity allows the designer and the homeowner wide latitude to produce a product that is pleasing to the eye, compatible with the neighborhood, and efficient in its operation. No structure has to be exactly like the house next door. In fact, most homeowners want to have a house that is distinctive in some way and exhibits in its design the lifestyle and outlook of the homeowner.

Creativity and imagination allow that to happen.

Third, the designer should maintain an open mind. If you engage a designer who has "all the answers" and is unwilling to make changes, you will be unhappy with the results. On the other hand, by engaging a designer who works easily with you, is willing to listen to your ideas, recognizes you as the final decision-maker in the process, and is pleased to make whatever changes you desire (assuming these ideas are structurally sound), then the experience in home design will be a genuine joy. So be careful to look for a designer who is willing to make changes without undue opposition and argument.

The fourth characteristic to seek in a designer is the ability to prepare clear and understandable plans. If a set of plans prepared by a designer is unclear and not understandable, the subcontractors involved in the construction process will have difficulty interpreting the plans and knowing how to proceed. The set of plans should include drawings for all the systems of the home—framing, electrical, mechanical (plumbing and heating/air conditioning systems), truss and roofing layout, door and window schedules, and any other specialty systems that might be included in the home.

It is absolutely essential that you take several sets of plans, study them carefully and, for the sake of clarity, ask a friend associated with the construction business (residential or commercial) to review the plans and offer an opinion as to their clarity and ease of understanding. Add the comments of the friend to your Designer Selection Sheet for each designer evaluated.

PICKING AND CHOOSING

Now, how do we find this magician who will be all these people wrapped up into one package? Before we go any further, let me explain that, if you are in a hurry to get started or if you have sold your house and must move within a specific time frame, be sure to start your search for a designer in sufficient time to get the design and construction completed. A timeline on the actual design can be found later in this chapter, but for now, be aware that searching for the right designer will not be a matter of a day or two.

To help you with the research process, a Designer Selection Sheet has been provided in the Appendix. You will see that it offers space for the name, address, and phone number of the prospective designer, along with the evaluation criteria mentioned. Carefully read the instructions on the sheet before initiating your search. The completed sheet will provide an excellent profile of all prospective designers and will assist you in making the right decision.

A good starting point for finding a designer is among your own friends. You may have one or two friends who are architects, designers, or draftsmen. They may even perform these services as a side business. If so, begin by asking them if they might be interested in working with you on the design and construction of your home. If one or more might be interested, proceed by researching the characteristics outlined earlier in this chapter. Also ask for designs that might have been drawn for someone else in the recent past and evaluate these designs according to the criteria above. By all means, do not select a friend as your designer simply because the person is a friend and might provide a break on the design fee. If the person meets the criteria outlined and is satisfactory to you and provides a fee break as well, then you have saved more dollars in the cost of the home. However, be sure that the person has the capability not only to draw the plans but also to ensure that the plans are executed properly in construction. An additional caveat is to evaluate — even discuss with your friend — any adverse reaction the friend might have if he is not selected to draw your plans. You may want to make sure that no hard feelings are generated from the experience.

Another source of designer names would be

friends or acquaintances who have built a home within the past few years. Be sure to determine how far back you would consider residences the designer may have been involved with before discussing the project with any prospective designers. Obtain the names of the designers of your friends' homes and inquire as to how pleased your friends were with the experience and especially the results.

Yet another alternative is to go to a house that is under construction and find the plans for that house. Often a tube is provided by the contractor on the job site at or near the location of the construction permit. In the tube you will find a copy of the plans for the house. The plans are there for the convenience of the city or county building inspectors. On each set of plans is the name, address, and phone number of the firm or person who prepared the plans. Make note of the information and place a call of inquiry regarding the services available. You may wish to make an appointment with the person or firm and proceed with the process outlined above.

A fourth alternative is to inquire of any contractor friends you may have. Most people know at least one or two people in the construction business. Inquire from that person about the names of architects or designers with whom he has had contact or experience. Note the names, then research the addresses and phone numbers. Follow up that research with phone calls and possible appointments.

If there is a home builder's association office in your town, you may want to call that office and inquire of designers who might be associate members. While the association's members are primarily contractors or builders, each local association has "associate" memberships available for suppliers of materials and services affiliated with the home building business. These associate members include building materials companies, architects, designers, floor covering companies, and the like. Explain that you are in the process of constructing a home and are in the planning stage. You want to make contact with a

designer, evaluate his work, and make a decision. The association will be happy to provide the names, addresses, and phone numbers to you. There might be a modest charge for this service. However, the information will be well worth it.

Probably the most obvious source of information on home designers is the Yellow Pages of the local telephone book. Often a forgotten resource, the Yellow Pages offer information, albeit advertising, to guide the homeowner in selecting several prospective designers for his home. Look under headings such as "Architects," "Drafting Services," "Designers—Residential," and "Home Designing and Planning Services." Read the ads carefully and with a degree of skepticism. In some cases only a listing will be found. In these cases it is your responsibility to sort the listings and decide on the firms or persons you will call. Record the information on the Designer Selection Sheet included in this book. And as you make contact and evaluate each designer, complete the information on the Selection Sheet.

THE DESIGNER CONTRACT

As with other elements of the construction process, no work should be initiated by any subcontractor without a written contract. The contract should delineate all considerations applicable to the work specialty of the specific subcontractor. More will be written about these subcontractor contracts in Chapter 7. At this point, suffice it to say that no design effort should be begun without a written contract outlining the terms and conditions under which the designer will function. And, of course, these terms should be agreed upon by both the designer and the homeowner/self-contractor.

What the Contract Should Not Be

While the contract with the designer should be considered a legally binding document, it is certainly not necessary that it be prepared by an attorney. The contract can be prepared jointly between the homeowner and the designer and can be agreed upon jointly by the two parties and attested by two witnesses. Instead of two witnesses, you may want to have both signatures on the document notarized. (See the Appendix for a sample contract with a designer.) Before discussing its specific contents, let's review the "nots" of the contract.

1. The contract should not be a simple, brief statement. While the length of the contract does not ensure greater enforceability, brevity is not being sought for the sake of simplicity. The contract is, after all, a legal document which should be able to withstand the scrutiny of the court in the case of disputes. Therefore, brevity is not a primary goal.

2. The contract should not be a statement of the wishes and plans of the homeowner/self-contractor only or of the designer only. A contract is a bilateral or two-sided document requiring the agreement of two parties. Thus the contract should spell out the responsibilities of both parties and the terms and conditions under which those responsibilities will be fulfilled.

3. The contract should not contain an *estimate only* of design costs. The contract should be specific in the statement of a professional fee charged and should not contain any blank spaces or any "extras" over which the homeowner has no definitive control. Such "extras" could permit the cost of the design to escalate to an unacceptable point.

What the Contract Should Be

Now that we have reviewed what a contract should not be or contain, let's take a look at what it should contain and how it should be written. As the terms and conditions are described in the contract, it is necessary to indicate whether the effort will be solely that of the designer or simply a plan of assistance provided to the homeowner

by the designer. Take special note of the following elements of the contract and their characteristics regarding sole responsibility or assistance. The contract should contain, at a minimum, the following elements.

1. *The schematic design phase.* This phase is fundamental to all else that will follow, for it is the phase which essentially lays out the elements to be included in the home and forms a first review by the homeowner of his layout within the floor plan. It is this phase that establishes the conceptual scheme of the residence based on discussions which have been conducted as a part of this phase. The discussions provide the designer with the requirements of the homeowner. Requirements, in this context, are probably best described as "dreams"—the product of one or two brainstorming sessions with the homeowner. These requirements or "dreams" are listed without consideration of cost, difficulty of implementation, or any constraining or facilitating factors. The designer then prepares drawings and other documents illustrating the scale and relationship of these project components to meet the requirements that have already been discussed.

The drawing part of this phase should be the sole responsibility of the designer in consultation with the homeowner. It is a phase that will require several meetings in which the homeowner and the designer will jointly review alternative drawings prepared by the designer. The drawings are compared with the "dreams" mentioned by the homeowner, and the homeowner shares criticisms with the designer with respect to his reaction to the drawings. Suggested changes are noted, and the designer is prepared to return with the changes included in the next drawing or alternative drawings.

Anticipated estimates of the potential cost of the project should begin also at this point in the process. To wait on cost calculations can prove a psychological and sometimes an emotional disaster. The reason for financial considerations at this point is to avoid the homeowner continually including an element, construction design, or materials that will add so much cost to the project as to frustrate and discourage the homeowner. So the designer should project costs of construction with each alternative design he presents to the homeowner from this point on. Furthermore, when changes are requested, the designer must be in a position to estimate the additional cost that might be incurred with such a change or, conversely, the reduction in cost with such a change.

Do not underestimate the value of this part of the design phase. It may very well be the most important exercise of the entire process.

2. *The design development phase.* After the determination of the elements to be included in the structure and after the schematic drawing has been approved by the homeowner, then the designer must prepare the revised design studies for the approval of the homeowner. These designs will be preliminary to the final product and will be sufficiently detailed to submit to the homeowner for final approval or to an architectural review board, if the subdivision in which you plan to build has such a board. The studies in this phase consist of drawings that fix and describe the size and character of the project in terms of its form, function, and other essentials. A more detailed cost estimate is also prepared by the designer during this phase.

When the design studies are submitted to you, the homeowner, be sure that you study them carefully. They will form the basis upon which the final documents will be prepared. Any changes at this point do not cause you to incur any additional expense. However, once the final documents are prepared and construction is underway, changes in plans will likely result in an accompanying increase in cost. So it is vital that you take at least a day or two to review the design studies carefully to ensure their accuracy for use in the drawing of the final construction documents.

One important note that needs to be mentioned at this point is that it will be essential that you,

the homeowner, see and review any and all changes suggested on a final design studies draft. Do not depend upon the designer to take your suggested changes and incorporate them into a set of construction documents without first having you review and approve them. Remember, the design studies are the plans that will be used to prepare the detailed construction documents. Please make certain that the plans to be used in that preparation are the plans you have fully approved. The designer should require your signature on the final design studies, thus ensuring against a last minute change of mind or disagreement.

3. *The construction document phase.* After the preliminary work has been completed and the design studies have been approved and signed in a final form, i.e., no more changes have been suggested that are not included in the last set of design studies reviewed, then the designer is ready to draw the construction documents. These documents comprise a "set" which is used by the subcontractors for the actual construction of the residence and is based on the final approved design development studies.

The designer meticulously prepares these detailed drawings — sometimes called "working drawings." The set of documents contains the details of each system to be included in the home with accompanying specifications setting forth the requirements for the construction of the residence. Furthermore, the designer will provide, during this phase, a "probable construction cost" based upon the final design development studies and the general market condition in your area of the country.

The construction documents are important to the overall construction project for two major reasons. First, the construction documents are the plans submitted to the local building inspector's office of the governmental subdivision (city, county, or township) with jurisdiction over the project. If you live in the city limits, the city building inspector will be responsible. If you live in a township or county, the building inspector's office in the township or county will have the responsibility for the project. Whichever the case, you will be required to obtain a building permit, and that building permit will be issued by the building inspector's office based upon the construction documents you submit to that office. Therefore, it is extremely important that all elements of the construction documents be in the "set" and available for study by the inspector's office. "All elements" here refers to specific pages of plans related to framing, electrical, mechanical, and so forth. Any variation of the plans from the building codes being enforced will result in the refusal of the building inspector's office to issue a permit and an overall delay in the process.

As a corollary to the issuing of the permit, once the permit is issued and construction has begun, periodic inspections of the construction will be conducted by the building inspector. You should maintain at the job site an exact duplicate copy of the construction documents submitted to the building inspector's office for issuance of a permit. The purpose for maintaining such a set is for review by the building inspectors, if needed, as they make their inspections. The copy of the construction documents placed in the tube at or near the posted building permit *must* be an exact duplicate of those on file in the building inspection department.

The second reason for the importance of these documents is that they will be used by the subcontractors to construct the home. Inaccuracies in specifications, designs that are unworkable, or code violations in the plans which are not discovered until later will frustrate the subcontractors. So it is important that the subcontractors be able to read the plans easily, understand them, and proceed with the construction unimpeded.

4. *The bidding or negotiation phase.* If you feel afraid to tackle the job of building your own home, you may wish only to have it designed, after which you put the plans out for bids to local licensed residential contractors. If that is the case, the designer should include in his contract assistance services for obtaining such bids. He can also be of assistance in negotiating the most favorable construction contract, since he will probably be familiar with the local contractors, their reputations, and whether market conditions are such as to justify negotiation from the written bid amount.

If you are planning on functioning as a self-contractor, the designer will assist you in interpreting the plans for prospective subcontractors and materials suppliers. If a subcontractor has a question about the plans that you cannot answer, the designer should be available to provide that answer and explain the plans. He can also advise the subcontractor on the reason(s) an element in the plan may be drawn the way it is.

Because of his familiarity with the materials market, the designer can advise you on whether the bids on materials are within market limits or if they are too high. This will help you identify good pricing structures from the suppliers. He can also help you compare the materials prices among suppliers, ensuring the greatest cost savings.

5. *The construction phase.* It is always advisable that the designer be available during the construction phase of the project. Periodic visits to the site will ensure that the project is being built according to the plans and specifications as outlined by the designer. Further, he can check on the quality of the materials as well as the quality of the construction and so advise the self-contractor. If discussions with the subcontractors are required as a result of his inspections, both the self-contractor and the designer should meet with the subcontractor in question and review the problems or the progress of the work.

Many times designers are reluctant to include this element in a contract. As a self-contractor, you *must* insist on its inclusion. This provision and its enforcement are your insurance against the use of materials and construction techniques with which you are unfamiliar.

Some designers will include the provision in the contract but charge an inordinately high fee for it. While this provision is paramount and should be included, its inclusion should not be grounds for charging a significantly higher fee.

6. *Fee structure and payment schedule.* All of the above-mentioned elements to be included in the contract are the responsibilities of the designer. The primary obligation of the homeowner/self-contractor is to ensure the timely payment of the fee being charged by the designer. Be sure that the contract contains a *total fixed fee.* You should be aware that some designers charge a percentage of the estimated cost of the residence. I do not recommend that method in this case primarily because, since you are self-contracting the house, its estimated cost will be difficult, if not impossible, to pre-determine. Therefore, in the absence of an estimate of savings over current market conditions, the designer will typically calculate his fee based solely upon current market conditions. So ask for a fixed fee from the designer. This will avoid "extra" charges and surcharges and keep the overall design cost to a minimum.

Ask that a payment schedule be included in the terms and conditions of the contract. You should not be expected to pay the entire amount of the contract at the beginning of the contract period, nor should the designer be expected to wait until he has completed the job to be paid. A progress payment plan is best suited to this type of project and typically would include a retainer to be paid to the designer at the signing of the contract with periodic payments due at the completion of each phase of the contract. Each progress payment is generally calculated as a percentage of the balance due after the retainer has been paid. (See the sample contract in the Appendix.)

7. *Signatures.* The final element to be written into the contract is space provided for signatures. The contract should be signed and dated by the designer as well as the homeowner (or one of the homeowners in the case of a married cou-

ple). While many states do not require witnesses for a contract to be enforceable, it is always advisable to have two witnesses to each signature or have the signatures witnessed by a notary public.

TIME FACTORS IN THE DESIGN PHASE

The design of a home is sufficiently important that it should not be hurried unnecessarily. Conversely, it is also not necessary to drag the exercise out beyond reason. The following schedule represents approximate time frames during which each of the three phases included in the design portion of the contract might be completed.

Schematic Design Phase	30-60 Days
Design Development Phase	20-30 Days
Construction Documents Phase	30-45 Days

A timeline of all the design phases and the construction phase is shown below.

Schematic Design Phase	Design Development Phase	Construction Documents Phase	Construction Phase

The importance of the three design phases of home construction cannot be overemphasized. And in light of that fact, there are two final factors that demand consideration.

The first of these factors is design control. Simply put: Who will control the final design of the home? As with many other endeavors, the person footing the bill usually has the final word in any matter. And so it is in the case of the homeowner/self-contractor. While the designer will play a prominent role in the project, he is not the final decision maker of the home design. The responsibility for the final design rests solely with the homeowner. After all, he is the person who will be living in and with the final result, possibly for a very long time.

The designer will work cooperatively with the

homeowner to ensure that the final plan and exterior design are in keeping with the wishes and dreams of the homeowner. He is the one who provides the necessary skill to see that the design is properly put on paper. But he is not the final judge of the product. Design control *must* be the sole responsibility of the homeowner.

A second factor demanding consideration is the implementation of the design. Most effectively executed, this is actually the joint responsibility of the self-contractor and the designer. The self-contractor will be supervising the construction project and will be overseeing the day-to-day progress of the job along with the construction manager. However, in accordance with the provisions of the contract, the designer will be conducting periodic inspections, preferably daily and in the afternoon, to ensure that the plans and specifications are being implemented properly. Any deviations from the plans or errors in construction discovered by the designer should be brought to the attention of the self-contractor for discussion with the subcontractor whose work is being questioned.

CONCLUSION

So we close this chapter the way we started—by saying that the key to getting a good start on a home is its design. Select your designer carefully. Early on, establish a good, working relationship with him. Work with him cooperatively in carrying out the plans he has painstakingly prepared. Pay him promptly when the progress payments are due. Commend him on his work, and allow him to take photographs of the finished product to show to future clients.

3

UNDERSTANDING THE TERMS
Speaking the Language

Every occupation I know of has words peculiar to its operation. You may have heard someone say, "Well, if you can speak the language you will do fine." We often call the language peculiar to an occupation or profession "buzzwords."

Probably no more important effort could be exerted by the self-contractor than to know, understand, and be able to use fluently the "buzzwords" of the construction industry. This chapter provides some of those buzzwords along with an explanation of their meaning and their relative importance to the process. You will find that many of these words are simply descriptive terms often used in the construction industry. Nevertheless, an understanding of and familiarity with these terms will endear the self-contractor to the prospective mortgage company considering the construction loan as well as to the subcontractors and the regulatory inspectors whose responsibility it will be to approve the construction. An understanding of the terminology conveys both self-confidence and an intelligent grasp of the process.

While the words in this chapter are being called "buzzwords," they really are nothing more than terminology used in the construction industry.

But if you as the self-contractor are not familiar with them, you will find yourself immersed in a sea of gibberish.

For the purpose of this chapter, the terminology is categorized into several groups. These groups represent the various stages, steps, or elements of the construction process and will allow you to refer to them easily. Furthermore, the words are in alphabetical order within each category for ease of reference.

PRECONSTRUCTION

The initial phase of the process is termed "preconstruction." It consists of those activities that make up the planning stage of the project. These terms or phrases will assist you in knowing how to plan, what to observe, and how to research.

ARCHITECT—Usually an individual with skills which have been specialized by training in either a college or a technical school. This individual will have undergone certain professional testing procedures, passage of which provides certification, which sets him apart in the field of construction design.

COVENANTS—Legal guarantees or restrictions (sometimes called "covenant restrictions") usually included in the recorded plat of a subdivision. They are typically limited by time in their effectiveness. For example, a restriction might be active and enforceable for a period of only thirty years. Such covenants might include setback lines, restrictions on the type of structures that can be built, minimum square footage, allowance or non-allowance of certain structures such as satellite dishes or outside clotheslines. Often the law requires that copies of subdivision covenants accompany any conveyance of a deed on a lot in a platted subdivision with recorded covenants.

DRAFTSMAN—An individual with special skills in design who may or may not have attended a college or technical school. This individual usually has not undergone the rigorous testing of the architect. An architect often begins a career in design by serving as a draftsman, functioning much like an apprentice. Fees charged by a draftsman would generally be less than those charged by a certified architect.

ELEVATION—A scale drawing or design of the exterior of a structure, especially front, back, and side views or perspectives. An elevation is drawn to provide an idea of how the finished structure will look on the outside.

HOME PLANNING SERVICE—A house design service, which often uses computers to design floor plans and elevations. Because of the computerization, a wide variety of options is available to the potential self-contractor.

PERMITS—Before any construction is allowed to begin, appropriate permits must be obtained from the regulatory agencies with jurisdiction over the construction of the house. If you live within the city limits of a municipality, then the city building inspection department is responsible for issuing the permits. If you do not live in the city limits, then the county or township would be responsible for issuing the construction permits. Construction permits are usually required by the local power company also before authorization of meter installation for a temporary power pole. If environmental concerns exist, the city, county, or township would require that such concerns be addressed and applicable permits from the environmental departments be issued before authorizing and providing a building permit.

FINANCIAL

One of the most difficult areas of construction to comprehend is the financial area. It will be your responsibility to convince the mortgagee or lending source that you have the capability to construct your own home. An understanding of the many terms and ideas related to the financial industry will go a long way toward convincing that lender that you actually know what you are doing. The following terms and phrases will assist you in getting a grasp of the loan process and the terminology associated with it.

ADJUSTABLE RATE MORTGAGE (ARM) — With a fixed rate mortgage, the interest rate is established for the life of the loan. However, with an adjustable rate mortgage, the interest rate can change throughout the life of the loan. These changes are periodic and are specified in the mortgage. The interest rate changes may be lower or higher, depending upon the movement of the index to which the interest rate is related. If the periodic interest rate changes, the monthly payment will change accordingly. Be sure to discuss the conditions and limitations on ARM's with each lender from whom you may seek financing.

AMORTIZE—This is a term used to describe the reduction of the principal of your loan over time. For example, when a mortgage payment is paid to the mortgagee, the payment customarily consists of three elements: the principal reduction amount, the interest payment, and, optionally, the escrow funds for taxes and insurance. As each payment is made, the principal is reduced by a calculable amount. In the beginning of the loan term, the principal of a fixed rate interest loan will amortize or be reduced by small amounts, while the interest will be the major portion of the payment. However, as the term of the loan progresses, the amount of principal reduction increases while the proportion of interest decreases. At the end of the loan term, the full principal amount of the loan has been repaid and the loan fully amortized or reduced to zero.

CLOSING COSTS — Sometimes called "settlement costs," these are the various amounts found on the Settlement Statement provided to you upon closing the construction and the permanent loans. There is an example of a Settlement Statement listing all the possible closing costs in the Appendix.

CONSTRUCTION LOAN — Financing a construction project is accomplished in two steps. The first step is the construction loan. This is an approved amount of money used to cover the expense of actually constructing the house. These monies may be used to pay for appraisals, surveys, materials, labor, permits, and other items directly related to the construction of the house. The construction loan often is extended or authorized at an interest rate higher than prevailing rates because it is of a short-term duration and is available on a draw basis. The construction loan is never considered to be permanent. Its purpose is fulfilled when the construction of the house is completed.

CONSTRUCTION/PERM LOAN — Some mortgage companies have a hybrid-type loan program under which you may be approved once for a loan which is used to construct the house and automatically converts to a permanent loan at the completion of construction. Be aware, however, that not all mortgage companies have this option, so you should inquire about it and especially about the conditions of such a loan when you begin shopping for financing.

DISCOUNT POINTS — Often these are simply called "points." "Points" are a one-time charge made by the mortgagee or lender to adjust the yield on a loan to what might be expected under market conditions and are the lender's way of "buying down" the interest rate. It is another way for the lender to provide yield for himself without increasing the interest rate on the loan. In fact, often discount points are quoted in conjunction with a specific interest rate. For example, a lender may inform you that you can obtain a mortgage at 9.0% interest, fixed, with 2 discount points. A discount point is equal to 1% of the mortgage amount. Therefore, if your mortgage amount is $50,000 and two discount points are charged, you will pay this one-time charge of $1,000 at closing.

ESCROW ACCOUNT — Typically, insurance premiums as well as property taxes are paid at specific times of the year, insurance in advance, taxes in arrears. However, it is important and expedient for the mortgage company to collect the funds for these items as a part of your mortgage payment. Therefore, the lender often establishes an escrow account, literally a trust account, into which that portion of your monthly payment that applies to taxes and insurance will be placed. The mortgagee estimates these amounts, collects the funds, and when the time of year arrives to forward the funds to the city or county and to the insurance carrier, the funds are available and paid out in a timely fashion. This escrow account is established to hold these funds until disbursement. In most cases, the lender is free to hold such funds in an interest-bearing account and may retain any interest realized on such funds.

FEDERAL HOUSING ADMINISTRATION (FHA)—This agency, which is a part of the Department of Housing and Urban Development, insures mortgages through lending institutions. Typically, the down payments required under FHA-insured loans are lower than conventional mortgages, and the interest rates may even be lower, depending upon market conditions. It is important to understand, however, that FHA does not loan money, it only insures the funds loaned by private lending agencies.

FIXED RATE MORTGAGE — These mortgages are characterized by a fixed interest rate over the life of the loan. The interest rate is not related to any index because no changes in interest rate, whether periodic or overall, are expected to occur. If the loan is for $50,000 over a twenty-five year period with a fixed rate of 9%, then the 9% interest rate will remain constant until the last payment in the twenty-fifth year.

INDEX—Lenders usually use some kind of index to determine the fluctuation of interest on adjustable rate mortgages. These indexes typically move up or down with the general movement of interest rates in the marketplace. Among the most common indexes used by lenders is the interest rate on one, three, or five year Treasury Notes. Another is the national, regional, or area average cost of funds to savings and loan associations. Some lenders will even use the cost of funds to themselves as the index for rates on ARM's.

LOAN DRAW—In order to make progress payments to the subcontractors or materials suppliers, it is necessary to have the funds to do so. A loan draw is a withdrawal of funds from the approved construction loan amount to be used to meet these expenses or progress payments as they occur. The loan draw is often based on a percentage of the work completed and is generally approved only after an inspection by an authorized officer of the mortgage company extending the construction loan. The loan draw is limited to the percentage of completion as determined by the mortgage company officer. Sometimes the mortgage company extending the construction loan will limit the number of loan draws without the payment of a fee. For example, a mortgage company may allow up to six draws without paying a fee for the draw; however, after six, you would be required to pay an inspection fee to the mortgage company for the privilege of making any draws over the six.

LOAN ORIGINATION FEES—These are funds charged by the mortgagee to cover the lender's administrative costs in processing the loan. Generally, as with discount points, the origination fee is charged as a percentage of the mortgage amount.

MORTGAGE — Legal evidence provided by a borrower in the form of a legally drawn instrument which secures the loan or note for the lender. Usually a promissory note, which gives evidence of the promise to pay, accompanies the mortgage.

MORTGAGE INSURANCE PREMIUM (MIP or PMI)—The lender may require you to purchase mortgage insurance protection. This insurance essentially protects the mortgagee from loss as a result of your inability to pay your mortgage payments. In many cases, the lender will make available higher loan amounts when mortgage protection is provided.

MORTGAGEE—The entity to whom a debt is owed, the lender, or the entity to whom a mortgage is pledged as security for a debt owed on real estate.

MORTGAGOR — The person who pledges a mortgage on the debt of real estate is considered a mortgagor. He or she is the borrower, the debtor, the individual, or the entity who owes the debt.

PERMANENT LOAN — When the house has been completed and certified for occupancy, the construction loan has fulfilled its purpose. At this point the permanent financial arrangements related to the house are prepared and closed. The permanent financing is the final loan, which will be amortized over the life of the loan.

Generally, permanent loan interest rates are lower than construction loan interest rates. But it is important to note that interest rates fluctuate on a daily basis. Therefore, it is possible to "lock in" an interest rate for the permanent loan within a specified period of time before the closing of the loan. So, if you think that interest rates will be lower nearer the time of closing the permanent loan, it is best *not* to lock in a rate. However, if you think that interest rates may be higher nearer the time of closing, you may wish to lock in an interest rate, which will be held for a specified period of time only.

PREPAID ITEMS — At closing, you will be required to pay in full certain items or at least partial payments. Interest from settlement to the first payment, mortgage insurance premiums, hazard insurance premiums, prorated city and county ad valorem (property) taxes, any annual assessments that might apply, and title charges are just a few examples of prepaid items that will require funds at closing.

RATE CAPS — Every adjustable rate mortgage (ARM) will contain conditions indicating the limit on interest rates that may be charged on a particular loan. This limit is called a "rate cap." It is simply a limit on the interest rates that can be charged. These caps are of two types: (1) Periodic caps, which place a limit on the amount of increase for one adjustment period; and (2) overall caps, which limit the interest increases over the entire life of the loan.

SECONDARY MORTGAGE MARKET—When a bank or financial institution extends a loan to an individual, the lender does not expect to hold that loan and mortgage for very long. Typically, whenever possible and in the shortest period of time, the lender will sell the loan and mortgage in the secondary mortgage market. This market is composed of private investors and federal agency investors who purchase the mortgages from the lenders. The two best known federal agencies that purchase mortgages on the secondary market are the Federal Home Loan Mortgage Association (FHLMA, commonly known as Fannie Mae) and the Government National Mortgage Association (GNMA, commonly known as Ginnie Mae). Among private purchasers in the secondary market would be insurance companies and private, individual investors.

VETERANS ADMINISTRATION (VA) — The Veterans Administration has a program through which it can guarantee the loans of qualified veterans who wish to build or purchase a home. Usually there is no down payment, an interest rate lower than most conventional mortgage interest rates, an assumable mortgage, extended amortization terms, and other considerations that make purchase by way of VA guarantees quite attractive. The VA will guarantee 60% of the loan amount up to a maximum of $27,500. However, that amount can be adjusted upward under certain conditions. If you are a veteran of military service, be sure to inquire as to the qualifications for VA financing.

CONSTRUCTION

During the construction phase, there are many terms and phrases that could be applicable. In this section, only a selection of the more important terms and phrases from among these many is provided. These terms and phrases are those of the greatest importance to the self-contractor. It is not essential that you be familiar with every detail of every construction activity, but it is vital that you be familiar with the common terminology used in this phase of the project.

The terms used in the construction phase are divided into two groups: (1) Materials and (2) Components. Each of these groups is listed separately.

Materials

The materials group consists of selected construction materials terms and phrases. These are listed to assist you in understanding how to negotiate for materials and to let the lender know that you are familiar with construction materials terminology.

DRYWALL—Most homes today do not use plaster on the walls and ceilings in the manner of thirty or forty years ago. The most common material is drywall, sometimes called wallboard, or gyp or gypsum board, and also known by a trade name, Sheetrock®. These boards, which typically measure 4 X 8 feet, 4 X 10 feet, and 4 X 12 feet, are hung with drywall nails, or sometimes screws, to the studs and ceiling joists of the framing. The seams are taped with a special paper tape and covered with "mud," a kind of spackling compound which is applied wet and dries to a hard finish. This finish can then be sanded smooth. The nail heads are also covered with "mud." After drying, the seams and nail heads are sanded and finished until the wall has a smooth texture.

EER—Heating and cooling systems are rated according to their efficiency. The EER, or Energy Efficiency Rating, is a measure of efficiency for these systems. The higher the EER, the more efficient the system.

FLASHING—Most roofs are not one uninterrupted surface. Often a roof is interrupted by vent stacks, chimneys, and other extensions into the deck of the roof. In the case of crickets and bay windows, the roof components must be attached to the wall or chimney. Flashing is galvanized sheet metal used around joints where these interruptions occur. The purpose of flashing is to prevent the intrusion of water around such interruptions, under the shingles, and into the house.

GFI—Water and electricity do not mix. Many building codes require the use of GFI-type receptacles when wall plugs are placed within a certain distance of a water source such as a faucet. GFI stands for Ground Fault Interrupter. The GFI wall receptacle contains a circuit breaker-type operation which, under certain conditions, will cause the circuit in the plug to open, shutting off electricity to the plug. The plug can be reset and power restored to the receptacle by the use of a button located on the plug itself.

GROUT—When ceramic tile is used in a house, it is installed by the application of adhesive grout. The grout also fills the joints between the tiles and provides for separation. Usually the grout is white; however, some house builders use colored grout to highlight certain features in bathrooms or floors.

GYPSUM BOARD—See DRYWALL.

LINTEL—When the exterior of a house is brick, it is necessary to have an "L" shaped support over the windows and doors on which the bricks can rest. This metal support is called a "lintel." It is generally made of metal approximately $1/8$ inch thick and is pre-cut according to the requirements of the opening; however, it may also be constructed of precast concrete.

LODGE POLE — This designation, which is shown on order forms as "LP," refers to soft, dense grain wood used in framing houses. The most notable use is as studs. Lodge pole lumber is either kiln- or sun-dried so that it is resistant to warping. Because of this dried characteristic as well as the uniformity and denseness of its grain, lodge pole lumber does not tend to react to weather conditions.

OXBOARD—Sub-flooring and roof decking may be composed either of individual strips of roof decking, plywood sheets, or sheets of oxboard. Oxboard is a composite material made of large wood chips in a heavy resin glue matrix. It can withstand the effects of water considerably better than plywood, which tends to separate when extremely wet or wet for an extended period of time. Oxboard is a durable material and can be treated, in terms of installation, like plywood.

PAINT FINISH—Wood materials and simulated wood materials are often mill-prepared for use only when the finish is to be opaque paint. Baseboards, doors and frames, chair rails, and other such trims may be milled by splicing together two or more pieces of the same trim design. The wood is then painted in such a way as to cover the wood grain and splicing joints. This is considered to be a paint finish.

PARQUET — Wood flooring consists of many types. Parquet is one of these types. It is a type of hardwood flooring which is usually installed in 6-inch squares using an adhesive material designed for that purpose. The parquet is versatile in design in that it utilizes parallel or perpendicular patterns. Complete installation requires that it be sanded, stained, finished, and waxed. It is possible to purchase parquet flooring which is pre-sanded and pre-stained.

PLYWOOD—When sub-floors and roof decking materials are purchased, plywood is one type of material to consider. Plywood consists of thin sheets of wood glued together or laminated to the desired thickness. The adhesive used in the gluing process is durable and strong. Plywood typically is purchased in 4 X 8 foot sheets.

PRESSURE-TREATED LUMBER—Certain materials in the construction of a house are required to be pressure treated against rot and pest infestation. The notation used to describe these pressure-treated materials is "PT." On an order for materials as seen in the Sales Estimate of Major Components in the Appendix, you may request fourteen 2 X 4 PT studs. This means that these materials would be pressure treated.

PVC—A form of plastic used to make pipes used in sewer and potable water lines. The initials stand for PolyVinylChloride, the chemical make-up of the material. Installation is much easier than with metal pipe since PVC is glued together.

R-FACTOR—Insulation, whether for ceilings or walls, is rated according to the insulation protection provided by the materials. This rating is called the "R-Factor." The higher the R-Factor, the higher the insulating capacity.

Insulation may be either blown, as in a ceiling, or in the form of fiberglass batts, as in a wall or ceiling. Where high levels of protection are required, such as a wall exposed to heavy sunlight, a higher R-Factor should be employed. But most important to remember is that the R-Factor does not relate to thickness of insulation but to the rating of insulating power. Typical R-Factors would be R-13 to R-19 in the walls of the home and R-19 to R-36 in the ceilings.

REBAR—Metal reinforcing rods placed in concrete to provide additional strength. The rods are manufactured in a variety of diameters to meet specifications in differing situations. Often small wire "rod chairs" are used to raise the rods off the dirt grade.

ROOFING SQUARE—The measure of roofing materials is generally in squares. A square is a 10 by 10 foot measure or 100 square feet of roofing material. Both roofing materials and roofing installation bids will be rendered and calculated in squares.

SOLDIERING—A form of brick-laying design in which the bricks are placed on end and mortared in place.

SOUNDBOARD—When a house is built in an area where noise is a common factor, such as an airport runway zone, the building codes often require the installation of soundboard at certain points in the house. Soundboard is fiber-type board which is applied to the outside of the framing members of the house as an added shield against the intrusion of noise.

STAIN FINISH—When wood trim materials or doors are stained and varnished in such a way as to expose the wood grain upon completion, the finish is said to be a stain finish.

STIPPLE FINISH — Most homeowners do not wish to have the walls look absolutely smooth. The most common finish installed in homes is the "stipple finish," which has the texture of orange peel. Blown on the walls, it provides a full texturization rather than a smooth or harshly rough finish.

THERMAL BREAK—An important achievement in any construction project is the effective insulation against heat and cold. This is achieved by the use of insulation in the walls and ceilings and by the use of thermal break or insulated windows. A thermal break window is characterized by two individual panes of glass separated by an air space which has been vacuum sealed. The separation of the glass panes forms a "break" against the changes in heat and cold.

TRUSS—In order to save time and money, today's builders use a truss system for roof framing and sometimes for floor framing in two- and three-story houses. Trusses are pre-fabricated framing systems for the roof and floors and are simply lifted and nailed in place by the framing subcontractor. These systems are computer-generated from the plans provided by you to the truss builder. Using the specifications from the plans, the trusses are fabricated and delivered, along with installation instructions, to the job site. While these systems are somewhat expensive to purchase, their cost is still less than would be required for hand-framing these components by a framing subcontractor.

VENTILATED SHELVING—Probably one of the more accepted forms of shelving in modern homes has been ventilated shelving. It consists of shelving components which appear as plastic or rubber sheathed wire attached to the walls by supports which are amazingly strong. Ventilated shelving can be used in many configurations and does not attract pests as with wooden shelving.

Components

The second element in the construction phase has to do with components of the construction. A knowledge of the components will go a long way toward helping you understand the various parts that comprise the typical home.

BALUSTER—The vertical supports for staircase railings are known as balusters. They are usually ornate, having been turned with a lathe to provide decorative trim for the staircase.

BATTER BOARDS—In laying out the foundation for the house, it is necessary to engage a surveyor to stake out the corners of the house. Out from these survey markers, heavy stakes are driven into the ground and horizontal 1 X 4 foot boards sighted, leveled, and nailed to the stakes as "batter boards." Strings are then attached to the batter boards to lay out the outside foundation walls and any inside reference markings.

CROWN MOLDING—Decorative molding attached to the wall at the point where it intersects with the ceiling.

FOOTINGS—The lowest portion of the house, which actually rests in the soils of the site, is a continuous, solid, reinforced concrete component known as the "footing." Footings are usually 12 to 18 inches deep and 12 inches wide. They form the most basic structure on which the entire weight of the house rests. In the case of a house being constructed off grade, footings consist of rectangular, poured concrete pillars on which pedestals or concrete block pillars or other materials rest.

FPM—In dealing with heating and air conditioning, the major element involved in the calculation of loads is the amount of air that the system can move over a specified period of time. That load factor is measured in FPM or feet per minute.

HEADER—The piece of lumber installed inside the house and as framing over doors and windows to provide additional strength over these openings is called a "header." Sometimes a framer will laminate, using nails, two pieces of 2 x 12 foot lumber and install the single laminated piece over doors and windows as a header to provide even more protective strength over the openings.

HVAC—This term refers to the Heating, Ventilation, and Air Conditioning system of the house. The term is taken from the first letters of each of these components.

JAMB—The frame to which a door is connected.

OFF-GRADE—The term "grade" is used to describe the ground upon which the house rests. Therefore, if a house is built "off-grade," then it is built on concrete blocks or some other type of piling off the ground. A floor joist system is used when the house is built off-grade.

PITCH — A roof is often characterized by its pitch. That is, the pitch describes the degree of slope on a roof over a specific measured linear distance. Thus a roof with an 8/12, said as an "eight on twelve pitch," indicates that the roof slope falls eight feet over a linear distance of twelve feet.

RIDGE VENT—At the point along the outside of the top of the roof where two roof decks intersect, a small opening is left to allow the ventilation of heated air from the attic areas. A metal cap, known as a "ridge vent," is used to cover this opening to avoid the intrusion of rain and other elements.

STUB OUT—The preliminary placement of all potable and waste water pipes prior to pouring a slab. The stub of the pipe is left above the level of the concrete slab for connection by the plumber later in construction or during trimout.

WAINSCOTING—Different decorative designs on a single wall. One design is usually applied up to a level of three feet and a different design applied to the area above. A chair rail is often used to separate the two distinctive designs.

LEGAL

In constructing a house, legal matters must be taken into account. Several items of interest legally should be noted and are explained here as terms with which you should be familiar.

ABSTRACT—Every piece of property has a history, some more colorful than others. A history of a property, which contains all the recorded information on file with the county, is called an "abstract" or "abstract of title." It contains such information as deeds, liens, transfers, deaths, mortgages, and other pertinent data to record the title history of the property.

CERTIFICATE OF OCCUPANCY — Once the house has been completed and the final inspection performed, the house is approved for occupancy. In order to certify legally the occupancy status of the house, the permitting governmental agency will issue a "Certificate of Occupancy." The certificate of occupancy authorizes the owner to occupy the house physically by moving in furniture and personal goods and having the power and other utilities connected. You can find an example of a "CO" in the Appendix.

LIENS—When a person owes a debt to another, the person to whom the debt is owed has the right to seek security for that debt. A "lien" or encumbrance may then be placed on the property of the debtor, recorded at the courthouse, and the "lien" serves as security for that debt. In the case of house construction, a lien may be placed on your residence by a subcontractor if you do not pay that subcontractor in full. Upon payment of the subcontractor, you may require that a Waiver of Lien form be signed by the subcontractor to ensure that the subcontractor has no legal recourse such as placing a lien on your property.

TITLE SEARCH—When property is transferred, it is necessary to ensure that the property is transferred free of encumbrances. A search of the title history of a property reveals such information. The cost of the service is a part of the settlement costs at closing.

CONCLUSION

This chapter has been designed to make the self-contractor familiar with terms and phrases he will come into contact with during the course of house construction. The contents are not designed to be all-encompassing or all-inclusive, but they do serve to familiarize the self-contractor with the more important aspects of house construction.

4

FINANCING
Obtaining Construction & Permanent Loans

Probably more time is spent agonizing over the dollars to be invested in building a house than any other element in the construction process. And that is understandable when one considers the enormous amount of capital being invested in a house. Typically, a home is the largest and most significant investment that a family makes during a lifetime. And since that is true, special care must be taken to protect that investment.

Few families have sufficient capital readily available to construct their dream house. Yet before actual construction is initiated, adequate funds must be available to complete the job. Since so few families possess the necessary capital in savings to accomplish the task, they must rely on lenders to provide such funds. This chapter outlines the process of seeking construction and permanent financing, explains the various types of financing available, describes in detail each element in the financing scheme, and offers advice on seeking and finding the most advantageous and attractive financing packages. Because they are a part of the process, pre-construction appraisals and construction insurance are also discussed in this chapter.

SEEKING HOME FINANCING

The number of mortgage companies has increased rapidly over the last few years. Time was when you wanted to build a house, you simply went to your local banker, who probably was a friend, and told him what you needed. He set the wheels in motion and approved and advanced the loan for your house. Well, times have certainly changed.

Today there is not just one bank in town, there are many, and all are making mortgage loans. And besides the banks, there are savings and loans that also provide home financing. In addition, there are mortgage bankers or companies making home loans which are subsequently sold to other investors for cash. And there are also mortgage brokers who, for a fee, seek mortgage packages to present to lenders for funding.

Let me elaborate on the last two of these sources, for it is critical that you know the difference between the two. Besides banks and savings and loans, there are mortgage *bankers* and mortgage *brokers* in the world of mortgage finance. The mortgage banker is a person or company whose business is to make and service loans. "Service loans" means to collect the monthly payment, pay the taxes when due, and pay the insurance premium when due. The mortgage banker seldom keeps the mortgage itself but rather sells it at a discount to interested investors such as banks, savings and loans, insurance companies, retirement trust funds, pension funds, and the like. Nevertheless, the mortgage banker has the final say as to whether the loan is made. Its sale in the "secondary market," the market in which loan originators sell their mortgages, is of little concern to the borrower. Often the purchaser of the mortgage in the secondary market will retain the mortgage banker to service the loan.

The mortgage broker is just that — someone whose business is to "broker" transactions or to seek out financing packages and present them to a lender. For this service he is paid a fee. Once the lender has been found, and the borrower and the lender have been introduced, the major part of the mortgage broker's participation has been completed. At times there may be additional pieces of information which the mortgage broker must obtain from the borrower, but once the loan package is in the hands of the lender, the broker's principal activity is concluded. For his services in bringing the two together, he is paid a pre-determined fee at the closing of the loan. No future servicing of the loan is the responsibility of the mortgage broker.

As a self-contractor, your primary interest is in obtaining a construction loan to assist in the payment of the subcontractors and suppliers of materials. Typically, mortgage brokers do not become involved in seeking lenders for construction loans. Note that the key word is "typically." There may be a few exceptions to that general rule, and you may wish to investigate several brokers during the course of seeking financing. However, the principal sources of construction financing will be banks and savings and loans. (In some states lenders will license a broker to represent the lender and thus the broker can also obtain construction financing.) You may wish to explore the possibility of construction financing with several mortgage bankers as well.

At this point, it is vital that you be aware that the financing you need to complete this project will actually consist of two phases, a construction loan and a permanent loan. And it is essential that you understand the difference between the two.

The first phase of the financing scheme is the construction loan. The construction loan is actually a mortgage of short-term duration provided to you to cover the cost of constructing your home. While the term of the loan varies with the mortgage company involved, it is generally for no more than twelve months, unless extenuating circumstances exist, say, for example, an estimated construction time of more than twelve months. The funds are made available on a "draw" basis, which means that periodic withdrawals from the loan fund can be made under certain conditions. Those conditions will be outlined later. Payments by the borrower are generally not made toward a construction loan, but interest payments are made monthly on funds drawn. When the construction of the home is completed, the permanent or long-term mortgage replaces the construction loan by paying off the lender of the construction funds.

The second phase in this scheme for financing your house project is the permanent loan or long-term mortgage. This is the loan which is actually repaid over time by the borrower. It is, in reality, a note promising to repay the lender and is collateralized by a mortgage on the property itself. The duration of this type of mortgage is generally lengthy, from fifteen to thirty years.

SOURCES OF FINANCING

Since you will be seeking financing for the construction of a residence, you will wish to make contact with all four types of financing sources noted above. The first source will be commercial banks. Generally, both construction and permanent financing can be obtained from a commercial bank. If you go to the commercial bank, you should first call for an appointment with a loan officer in the "residential mortgage" department. Sometimes it is called the "mortgage loan" department. Just make it clear that you wish to speak with someone about a residential loan.

When the time for the appointment arrives, be sure that you dress in clean, neat attire. At the appointment, clearly explain that you wish to perform as a self-contractor to construct your own home, and the purpose of this visit is to obtain information regarding construction and permanent loans available through the bank. Then allow the loan officer to explain to you the policies of the bank regarding self-contractors as well as the various types of loan programs available. Repeat this process at as many banks as you wish to contact. Using the Loan Information Guide in the Appendix, make notes in sufficient detail to refresh your memory later as to the information received from the specific bank.

The second source of loan funds is the savings and loan bank. These banks, sometimes known as "thrifts," are in the business to provide residential mortgage financing. In fact, the savings and loans of the United States are the single largest provider of residential mortgage loans in the country.

The manner of making contact with the savings and loan is much the same as that of the commercial bank. In a small savings and loan organization, you may speak only with a loan officer. In the larger savings and loan institutions, residential mortgage or mortgage loan departments will operate, and you will want to speak with a loan officer attached to this department. From this point, the procedure for contact, appointment, and evaluation is the same as that related to commercial banks above.

The third source of loans is the mortgage banker. This is a person or a corporation who actually lends money and services loans. You will generally find mortgage bankers listed under "Mortgages" in the Yellow Pages of the telephone book. Often you will find in the advertisements a statement that the firm is a "licensed mortgage banker." When that statement appears, you know that the company itself is in the business of lending money. However, be aware that, often, mortgage bankers do not lend construction monies, only monies for permanent financing.

Since the sole business of these companies is to lend money and there will be no separate department for mortgage loans, you may wish to call and simply make an appointment with a loan officer. Meet that appointment and complete the information on the Loan Information Guide.

The final source of loans is the mortgage broker. The mortgage broker is a person or corporation who does not lend money directly but puts you in touch with a bank, savings and loan, mortgage banker, or private investor who does lend money directly. For this service the mortgage broker is paid a fee. You will find listings for a wide variety of mortgage brokers in the "Mortgages" section of the Yellow Pages. You need to remember that these people do not lend money directly and, sometimes, cannot secure construction financing for you. There are, on the other hand, mortgage brokers who can secure both construction and permanent financing.

One important word of caution should be noted at this point. When you meet with the loan officer seeking information on loans, terms and conditions, and loans to self-contractors, be aware that you will likely be told that the policy of the institution is not to make construction loans to "homeowner-contractors." And it may very well be true. But take the case of the bank that provided the construction loan on my house. The policy manual of this bank reads: "Loans to Individuals to Build Their Own House . . . As a general rule, *Don't Make Any*." Yet, this very bank provided both construction and permanent financing for my house. The lesson learned is simple. When the banker says, "We make no loans to homeowners to build their own houses," just smile, say, "OK," and continue to gather the information needed to evaluate financing sources.

TYPES OF FINANCING PROGRAMS

Over the years, the complexity of home mortgages has changed dramatically. When my mother and father built a home in 1939, they went to a local savings and loan association, borrowed $5,000 at 2% interest for a period of thirty years, and paid monthly payments of $26. With the addition of taxes and insurance, the monthly payments reached $35 per month. Simple arithmetic. No complicated formulas, just borrowing a fixed amount, at a fixed rate, for a fixed period of time.

But times have become somewhat more complicated than that. Because inflation and the prices of homes have escalated more rapidly than the incomes of many Americans, new programs of financing had to be developed. New approaches to financing the "American dream" were created, until today there is a financing scheme for almost everyone. In this section, we will review several of these programs in detail and mention a few of the others. By no means is space available to discuss in detail all the financing programs available through the banks, savings and loans, and mortgage bankers.

Construction Loans

As a self-contractor, this is probably the most important transaction in which you will become involved—securing construction financing. It is the scale on which will be balanced the decision of the mortgage company against your actual ability to self-contract your home. Thus it is vital that you take careful note of the information included in the section on applying for a loan later in this chapter.

Construction financing is the foundation on which the house will be built, for it provides the resources to pay the necessary costs incurred in the construction. And as the proposed self-contractor, you will be required to convince the lender that you are capable of serving as a self-contractor without high risk to that lender.

No financing institution will make a loan, construction or otherwise, to someone in whom they do not have utmost confidence. After all, the company is in the business to make money, and it will not take a risk greater than the risk taken when a licensed residential contractor is involved. So you must raise the comfort level of the financing institution sufficiently that the lender will provide the construction loan without question or hesitation.

Construction loans are generally obtained from either a commercial bank or a savings and loan institution. The construction loan will typically be for no more than 75 to 80% of the pre-construction appraised value. This pre-construction appraisal represents the value the appraiser projects the house and lot to be worth upon completion of the structure. The appraisal does not take into account any savings on the construction by virtue of your acting as a self-contractor. The value is considered to be the fair market value of your house, in that neighborhood, at the time of completion. This appraisal is based on a value per square foot as determined by comparable sales in the general area in which your home is located. If comparable homes in your area sell for $65 per square foot and you can construct your house for $35 per square foot, the savings is obvious.

Some lenders restrict the construction loan amount to 75 to 80% of the actual "cost" of construction as established by a written cost estimate provided by the borrower/builder. The lender then often provides a copy of the cost estimate to the appraiser and requires a statement from the appraiser that the cost estimate appears reasonable.

The interest rate the construction loan bears will vary with the financing institution. However, it is often one to two percentage points above the prevailing prime rate, which changes on a daily basis. The maturity period of construction loans varies from six to twelve months, depending upon the extensiveness of the construction. Construction loans with greater periods of maturity are available for larger, more complex, and time-consuming residential projects.

Whether or not the loan is a percentage of the pre-construction appraised value of the cost as determined by builder cost estimate, the value of the lot will be integrated into the "cost" of the project. As a general rule, if the lot has been owned for less than one year, the price paid for the lot is used (assuming the lot is not appraised lower than the price paid). If the lot has been owned for more than one year, the appraised value will be used. If the lot is being purchased simultaneously with obtaining the construction loan, the lower of the price or value will be used.

I can hear you saying, "Wow! I don't even have to put anything into the project to get the construction funds." Not so. The financing institution will require that you have equity or an equal share (this could be liquid assets available) equivalent to 20 to 25% of the final construction loan amount. If the amount being borrowed as a construction loan is $120,000, the bank will require that you have equity or funds available equal to $24,000, assuming an 80% construction loan.

This equity may take the form of a residential lot on which no money is owed, cash, or other liquid assets which will be assigned to the project. In either case, the lender is interested only in the fact that you have a vested financial interest in the project.

A relatively recent development in the financing of construction projects has been the availability of construction-permanent loans, sometimes called "construction-perms." These programs have the potential not only for advantageous opportunities but for fearsome nightmares. The program typically consists of a one-time closing, with savings being realized on the origination fee on a permanent loan, the fee for recording the mortgage, and duplication of mortgage title insurance issuance.

This kind of mortgage is described quite accurately by its name. It consists of a construction loan which, upon completion of the project, automatically rolls over to a permanent loan with a scheduled amortization. And because of its nature, it is a loan made to a borrower, not to a builder. Origination fees and discount points vary widely in these programs, so it is important that you investigate, with caution, the provisions of any construction-perm you might consider.

No effort here will be given to describing all forms of construction-perm, but we will provide information on three types to illustrate their activity.

1. Adjustable rate construction-perm loan. This type of loan has a floating rate in force during the construction period based upon the activity of the prime rate. After completion of construction, the loan converts to a permanent loan with an adjustable rate determined by the activity of a readily available public index such as the yield on U.S. Treasury securities. In some cases, these loans include provisions that allow for conversion to a fixed rate during the second through the fifth years. Rarely is the conversion option offered after five years. This option to convert to a fixed rate is not a general rule but is sometimes included. You will want to clarify that provision with your loan officer if this type of construction-perm loan is used. Be aware that the construction portion of any of the three types of construction-perm will often be like any standard construction loan, that is, one to two points over the prevailing prime rate. And that interest rate changes on a daily basis, therefore, the interest rate on the construction portion of the loan will also change. Note, however, that some construction-perm loans offer the same rate during the construction as well as the permanent portion of the loan.

2. The second type of construction-perm provides for the rate on the permanent loan to be established at the time of approval of the construction-perm. This can be a fixed rate or an adjustable rate; however, this rate applies only to the permanent portion of the loan. While this provision may have its disadvantages in terms of falling interest rates, it can also be advantageous to the borrower in a time of widely fluctuating interest rates, especially if, at the completion of construction, the interest rates have increased. The construction portion of the loan functions as mentioned above.

3. The third type of construction-perm program consists of a construction loan advanced at one to two percentage points over the prime rate with the permanent loan being determined by a loan modification agreement with a fixed rate. This allows the financing institution to use the rate in force at the time that the permanent loan becomes activated.

As a part of the construction loan application process, you will be asked by the lender to justify your request by completing an estimate of costs. A form, which may be used for that purpose, Borrower's/Builder's Estimate of Costs, is included in the Appendix. This estimate of cost will be provided to the pre-construction appraiser for evaluation as to reasonableness.

The closing procedure for a construction loan is not unlike that of any permanent real estate loan. Standard notes, deeds, mortgage loan agreements, and other legal documentation are required to close the loan. Title binders or title policies may be required along with a certified survey of the real estate. In the case of the self-contractor, evidence of builder's risk and/or general liability insurance most likely will also be required. More will be mentioned about insurance later in this chapter.

Once the construction loan has been closed, you are ready to begin the construction process. As you need funds for the construction, "draws" or "advances" may be requested from the bank.

Each draw generally must be approved by an officer of the department before the draw is actually disbursed. That approval is contingent upon an on-site inspection by the officer approving the draw or someone else authorized to conduct the inspection and approve the draw. The draws are typically approved based on a percentage of completion as determined by the on-site inspection. The Construction Loan Disbursement Schedule in the Appendix illustrates the typical draw process and the percentage estimates of completion for each increment of construction.

As a self-contractor, you must be careful to time your draws of funds properly. The tendency might be to make draws of funds not yet needed, and you might be tempted to use unexpended funds for purchases other than construction. Therefore, I advise that minimum funds be maintained and that your draws be scheduled to provide for timely payment of construction costs, yet without keeping a large balance in the account. Remember, you are paying interest on amounts actually disbursed by the lender. You do not wish to pay interest on funds not yet needed. If you establish a separate account for the disbursement of these funds — and you are advised to do so — try to put them in an interest-bearing account. The monies that may remain in the account will at least be earning interest.

Permanent Loans

As mentioned above, as economic times have changed, so has the world of home financing. While a few of the standard-type loans are still around, generally speaking the kinds of permanent loans available today are quite different from those of forty years ago.

The basic types of loans available from lending sources are (1) loans guaranteed by the Federal Housing Administration/Veterans Administration and (2) conventional loans. An explanation of these types follows.

FEDERAL HOUSING ADMINISTRATION/ VETERANS ADMINISTRATION LOANS

Many people believe that the Federal Housing Administration, better known as FHA, and the Veterans Administration, VA for short, are in the mortgage lending business. Nothing could be further from the truth. FHA/VA are federal agencies that *insure* mortgage loans issued by FHA- and VA-approved lenders. These agencies do not lend money directly.

Note especially that these loans are not available through every financing institution. They are only available through those lenders approved by FHA or VA. Furthermore, FHA and VA loans are available only on homes built according to plans and specifications outlined by FHA and VA. While these plans and specifications may, and I emphasize *may*, be less strict than the plans and specifications of your proposed house, nevertheless, FHA and VA will require that the plans and specifications conform to the requirements of these agencies.

There are advantages to securing financing from lenders with guarantees from FHA and VA. Among these advantages are: (1) a moderate interest rate; (2) reduced down payment in the case of FHA, and often no down payment in the case of VA; (3) an extended amortization or repayment period; and (4) generally, no prepayment penalty.

If you wish to secure an FHA or VA mortgage on your proposed house, you will be required to submit a detailed set of construction plans to FHA or VA for approval. In addition, during the construction phase, FHA or VA compliance inspectors will periodically inspect your house to ensure that it is being constructed according to the plans and specifications outlined and the standards required by FHA or VA.

CONVENTIONAL LOANS

Conventional loans are loans offered by lending institutions and require no approval by a government agency for lending purposes. The banks, savings and loans, or mortgage bankers may solely make the decision to advance the loan to you. There are a number of types of these mortgages, and the financial community is constantly reviewing these types and evaluating additional types to offer to the borrowing public. For the sake of space and time, we will review the concepts of only a few of the various types of mortgage repayment plans available.

Fixed Rate Mortgage—This is the mortgage my mother and father would have been familiar with. A specified amount of money is borrowed over a long term, usually twenty-five to thirty years, with the mortgage balance being amortized or reduced during that period. The interest rate is fixed at the beginning of the life of the mortgage, hence the name "Fixed Rate Mortgage," with the monthly payments remaining equal during the term of the mortgage. At the beginning of the mortgage term, larger portions of the monthly payment apply to interest with a smaller portion applied to reducing the principal of the loan. However, the longer the payments are made on this loan, the greater the amount applied to principal and the lesser the amount applied to interest. At the end of the term, the mortgage is paid off.

Adjustable Rate Mortgage—This instrument is a loan in which the interest rate is not fixed but changes over the lifetime of the loan in relation to the movements of a specific index rate. It is sometimes referred to as an "adjustable mortgage loan" or a "variable rate mortgage." Typically, the interest rates charged at the beginning of the life of an ARM are lower than those for fixed rate mortgages; thus at times, you may qualify for a loan of greater amount, since the repayment schedule is based upon current income.

ARM's have become popular in the last few years because they do offer advantages for those in the early stages of a career or for those whose income potential is greater than current actual income. However, when considering an ARM, the Federal Reserve Board, in a pamphlet entitled *Consumer Handbook on Adjustable Rate Mortgages*, states that you might wish to consider the following questions:

❏ Is my income likely to rise enough to cover higher mortgage payments if interest rates go up?

❏ Will I be taking on other sizable debts, such as a loan for a car or school tuition, in the near future?

❏ How long do I plan to own this home? (If you plan to sell soon, rising interest rates may not pose the problem they do if you plan to own the house for a long time.)

❏ Can my payments increase even if interest rates generally do not increase?

When considering financing programs for your house, investigate all the possibilities. You might wish to submit the Mortgage Checklist in the Appendix to the various loan officers for a comparison. You can then take the information and make an informed judgment as to the advantages for *you* regarding the types of financing available.

Term or Straight-term Mortgage—This type of instrument allows the borrower to make interest-only payments during the life of the mortgage, with the final payment (called a "balloon payment") retiring the principal portion of the mortgage. Note that during the life of the mortgage, the principal balance is not reduced, only interest payments made, usually on a quarterly, semi-annual, or annual basis. The typical term for such a mortgage is three to five years.

Graduated Payment Mortgage — This instrument is a long-term loan whose main characteristics include a fixed interest rate over the life of the mortgage and a variable payment plan. Under this type of loan, the monthly payments increase by a specified percentage rate each year until the payment reaches a pre-specified level. When that level is reached, the monthly payments no longer increase but remain constant

for the remainder of the life of the loan. This program is especially good for younger borrowers whose incomes will only allow them to make smaller monthly payments but with the potential for larger payments later in their careers.

This section is, by no means, intended to be a capsule summary of all mortgage loan types available. It does, however, illustrate that you should investigate carefully as many options regarding loan repayment plans as possible before entering into the loan application process.

APPLYING FOR A LOAN

Before any explanation of the loan application procedure is shared, allow me this brief paragraph to help you recognize the critical nature of the financing process. As a prospective self-contractor—at this point you are still a *prospective* self-contractor—you will be required to prove yourself before any financing agency will lend you money to construct your home. It will be necessary that you prove:

❏ that you have sufficient knowledge of the construction process to complete the project;

❏ that, unless you have extensive knowledge of and experience in construction, you will have someone who does have such knowledge and experience assisting you;

❏ that you will be prudent in the handling of all funds associated with the project;

❏ that you at least appear to know what you are doing.

The financing agency, whether a bank, a savings and loan, or a mortgage banker, is in the business to make money. It is not the intent of this agency to make loans to those who may not be able to carry through on a project. And, parenthetically, this is also true with respect to licensed residential contractors who have "fly-by-night" reputations. The agency will carefully question and investigate you to determine your level of competence to finish the job. Therefore, you have the responsibility to *sell yourself*. And the place to begin selling yourself is at the very beginning.

The First Appointment

With the Loan Information Guide form in hand, proceed to the appointment with the loan officer. While you are not really trying to pretend to be somebody or something that you are not, it is vital that you convey an attitude of self-confidence and self-assurance. To that end the following admonitions apply:

Be on time. It is far better that you wait on the loan officer than that the loan officer have to wait on you. You may be saying, "Well, my time is valuable too, so if he has to wait a few minutes on me, why should that cause a problem?" You are probably right in terms of the equal value of time. But, after all, you are coming in to ask for money, and he certainly does not have to give it to you. So don't bring unnecessary pressure to the situation by being late for an appointment.

Be sure to dress appropriately, in a manner that conveys to the officer an attitude of confidence.

Present yourself with self-assurance. Body language can speak volumes to an observant loan officer. Therefore, do not slump in a chair, smoke, or have your attention drawn from the immediate situation. While you may not be in control, at least appear to have control of the situation.

Do not be argumentative. If you do not agree with some statement that the loan officer makes, do not argue. After all, he may be right. It is certainly better to be agreeable, even if the officer is wrong, than to be disagreeable and have him be right. After all, a wrong word not spoken can achieve much.

Listen attentively. The information provided by the loan officer will be important. It is crucial that you listen carefully to all that he has to say. Make detailed notes on the Loan Information Guide as the loan officer speaks. Your note-taking will also convey an attitude of attentiveness.

Thank the loan officer for his or her time. Much can be achieved by a simple "thanks." Then tell the loan officer that you will make contact again later. If you have the time, you may even wish to write a letter to the loan officer thanking him for his time and information and reiterating that you will maintain contact.

Evaluation of the Loan Information

After you have contacted as many financing agencies as you feel is necessary, begin a careful study of the data and notes on the Loan Information Guide. From these data and notes and based upon your needs, determine the best source of funds for your project. That determination should be based on several criteria among which are:

❏ whether the institution provides construction loans or permanent loans only

❏ the interest rate history of the institution over the immediate past two years

❏ the discount points to be charged

❏ the amount of any origination fees that might be charged

❏ the general impression given by the loan officer toward you as a self-contractor

❏ the availability and advantages of construction-perm loans

❏ the ease of obtaining draws, i.e., how quickly you will be able to obtain funds during the construction phase

❏ the frequency of draws available during the construction loan phase

❏ the time frame for approval of your loan package

❏ the complexity of the loan package.

These "tests" are by no means all-encompassing. They are simply a guide to help you determine the most suitable financing institution for your project. There may be other determining factors you want to consider. Such factors are different for different people. The most important consideration, however, is that you collect adequate data and notes from the prospective financing institutions and use those data and notes to ascertain the appropriate institution to meet *your* specific needs.

The Second Appointment

After you have decided which financing institution you want to approach for your financing needs, call the loan officer with whom you met the first time and set a second appointment. Explain that you would like to discuss seriously the application process and set that process in motion as soon as possible. When the appointed time arrives, go to and conduct the second meeting in exactly the same manner as the first meeting. The same admonitions listed as confidence-building and the exhibition of self-assurance apply also to this second meeting with the loan officer. *Keep them in mind and heed them!*

At this second appointment, you and the loan officer will get down to what might be called the "nitty-gritty." The application process will be reviewed and all the appropriate application papers will be provided to you for completion. The conditions of the application process will also be explained by the loan officer at this time.

Be patient. The loan officer's job is to make certain that you are aware of the pitfalls of mortgage applications and the variety of results that might occur. He is doing his job. He is required to protect your rights as a borrower and to make sure that you are informed regarding the various rules and regulations of lending and trade practices. Be sure to set aside enough time to review all this material with the loan officer carefully. I would suggest a minimum of one to one and one-half hours for this meeting.

When you leave the loan officer, you should be armed with all the necessary paperwork you will have to complete. In fact, he may have provided you with pre-packaged materials with instructions enclosed explaining every detail requiring completion. You are now ready to begin the application process.

The Mortgage Loan Application Package

You now have the application package, which will provide the mortgage company sufficient data to determine whether a loan will be approved for your construction project. Complete the application with care and make absolutely certain that all forms required by the mortgage company are complete and clearly written. Do not try to save time by skipping portions of any of the forms. Such actions will only cause a delay in the decision-making process.

The mortgage application package will require the completion of several types of forms and the provision of certain confidential information. The first form to be completed will be the application itself. Many mortgage companies use the Federal National Mortgage Association (Fannie Mae) Form 1003. You will find a copy of this form in the Appendix.

This form is not complicated and should be printed, in ink, with legible handwriting. No section of the form should be overlooked or skipped. Every item should be addressed even if it does not apply to you. If the item does not apply to your situation, an "X" should be drawn through the response box or "N/A" written in the space provided.

Often it is difficult to know exactly what information is called for on an application such as the mortgage application form. Therefore, I have provided in the Appendix a Home Loan Application Checklist to aid you in knowing what specific information is being requested in each section. Use this checklist as you complete your application form to ensure accurate data. One word of caution, however. If your loan officer provides you with a different kind of checklist or requests information different from that shown in this book, you must comply with the requirements of the lender and supply the specific information requested by that mortgage company in precisely the form requested. All the information contained in this book is simply to familiarize you with the process so that you do not lessen your chances of obtaining a loan.

The mortgage company *may* require the submission of other paperwork to make the loan application file complete. While the requirements differ with each mortgage company, among the forms required by some companies are:

❑ General Authorization Form for the verification of employment and credit information

❑ Appraisal Request Form for the pre-construction appraisal

❑ Sales Contract on the property if you already own the lot on which you plan to build the house.

In addition to these forms, the mortgage company will require the prepayment of certain fees. Generally these fees are for the pre-construction appraisal by an appraisal company of the mortgage company's choosing and for a credit report, both of which items become a vital part of the application package.

A final but most important piece of information required by the financing institution is a set of the house plans. While the requirements may differ among the finance companies, generally a set of plans drawn during the design development phase will suffice. The plans must, however, be the final draft prepared in the design development phase. Any changes in the plans after submission to the financing institution will require notification both to the financing institution and to the appraiser who conducts the pre-construction appraisal. Be sure to check with the loan officer as to which set of plans he requires, whether a set from the design development phase or a set of the final construction documents.

Now the hard part begins — the waiting. You have meticulously prepared your application package, and all documents are in place. The loan officer has confirmed that all documentation is complete and that the bank will be obtaining the additional information, that is, the pre-construction appraisal and the credit report, as soon as possible. Upon receipt of this additional information, the loan committee will consider your loan. *Be patient!* This part of the process may take as much as three weeks, depending upon the institution, the number of loans being considered, the backlog of work, and the receipt of the additional information. But the answer *will* come.

Suddenly, one day, the telephone rings, and the loan officer tells you that your loan has been approved. All that remains is for a closing to take place.

COSTS ASSOCIATED WITH LOANS

No amount of money is ever borrowed without accompanying costs. Sometimes the novice borrower will be unaware of these costs, sometimes called settlement or closing costs. In the Appendix is a copy of the Settlement Statement approved by the United States Department of Housing and Urban Development. A Settlement Cost Worksheet for determining the settlement charges you might incur with your loan is also included.

In 1974, Congress enacted the Real Estate Settlement Procedures Act (RESPA), which was designed to protect the consumer by enlightening the consumer of the process of settlement and the nature of any charges incurred. A part of the loan application process includes a requirement of the lender to provide a Good Faith Estimate of the costs of settling the loan for which you have applied. And since there is no standard settlement process throughout the country, both the process and the costs incurred may vary from area to area.

The following section contains information from a brochure entitled *Settlement Costs* produced by the Office of Housing and Urban Development. It provides an overview of the settlement services that may be required and for which you may be charged.

LOAN ORIGINATION FEE — This is a fee lenders charge to defray the administrative costs in processing the loan. The fee is generally described as a percentage of the total loan amount and will vary among lenders and localities.

LOAN DISCOUNT POINTS—Lenders are in the business to make money. When interest rates decline, often discount points will increase to make up for the loss of revenue from interest and to offset the constraints often placed on the lending institution by state and federal regulations. It is a one-time charge paid at closing and is simply the lender's way of "buying down" the interest rate. A "point" is the equivalent of 1% of the total loan or mortgage amount.

APPRAISAL FEE—This is a fee applied to the cost of obtaining an estimate of value from a residential appraiser at the time the loan is obtained. An appraisal is necessary to ensure that the value of the home, or the anticipated value of the completed home in the case of construction loans, will exceed the loan value by at least 20% where an 80% construction loan is being considered. In the case of a construction project, a pre-construction appraisal will be conducted, for which an appraisal fee will be charged. Upon completion, a final inspection will be made by the appraiser to verify the satisfactory completion of the structure. This appraisal is certified by the appraiser with the Satisfactory Completion Certificate shown in the Appendix. The lender also may charge a fee for this final evaluation.

CREDIT REPORT FEE—This fee covers the cost of obtaining a credit report indicating how you have handled other credit transactions in which you have been involved in the immediate past.

LENDER'S INSPECTION FEE — Some lenders charge fees for having their personnel go to the job site and inspect in anticipation of a draw from the construction loan. Other lenders permit a certain number of draws at no cost to the borrower with any inspection above that number charged to the borrower at a pre-set amount.

INTEREST—Lenders typically require that you pay interest on your loan for the period between closing and the first payment. These interest charges are calculated on a per diem basis and are charged only on amounts actually disbursed.

MORTGAGE INSURANCE PREMIUM — You will be required by the lender to obtain mortgage insurance. This insurance protects the lender from loss due to the default of the borrower. The premium may be paid in a lump sum, in advance, or the lender may require only that the first premium be paid. In the case of lump sum payment, said payment covers the lifetime of the loan. Please make sure that you are aware of the time period covered by the mortgage insurance policy. While it may cover the entire life of the mortgage, it may also be in force for only a portion of the life of the mortgage. Note, however, that generally mortgage insurance is not required if sufficient equity is available, e.g., loan to value ratio of 80% or less of estimated cost including the lot.

HAZARD INSURANCE PREMIUM—Generally the first year's premium is required as prepayment for hazard insurance. It is a homeowner's policy which insures against losses due to fire, windstorm, other natural hazards, personal liability, and theft. If you are in a flood-prone area, your homeowner's policy may not cover loss due to flooding. You will then need to contact the Federal Emergency Management Agency for information regarding the National Flood Insurance Act.

PEST INSPECTION FEE—A fee will be charged for the purpose of inspecting the structure for the presence of termites or other types of pest infestation.

CITY/COUNTY PROPERTY TAXES—A reserve account is established for deposit of these funds at closing. You will be required to prepay all taxes that will become due between the closing and tax payment time. When payment is due, then the taxes collected at closing and placed in escrow are forwarded for payment to the appropriate governmental subdivision.

ANNUAL ASSESSMENTS—If you live in an area which has incurred the cost for certain improvements, i.e., sidewalks, sewers, paving, and the like, you may be required to pay your pro rata share of the assessments.

TITLE CHARGES—These fees may include the costs of title examination, title search, document preparation, title insurance, and legal fees. The title action on your transaction is important because it will determine whether there exists a clear title to the property and will disclose any issues on record that might adversely affect clear title. Such issues might include unpaid mortgages, judgments or tax liens, conveyance of mineral rights, leases, power line easements, road rights of way, or other matters that might limit the use and enjoyment of the property.

ATTORNEY'S FEES—Occasionally legal fees will be incurred in connection with a transaction. You may be required to pay all or a portion of these fees in connection with your loan.

GOVERNMENT RECORDING AND TRANSFER CHARGES — Typically, charges are levied for the purpose of recording deeds, recording mortgages, and governmental tax collections such as documentary stamps. These are collected at closing.

Some of these fees are not collected at the time you close a construction loan. A few of these fees are collectible only at the closing of a permanent loan. However, fees such as the loan origination fee, discount points, appraisal fee, credit report fee, lender's inspection fee, and attorney's fees may be payable upon the closing of a construction loan.

Pre-Construction Appraisals

One fee charged to you will be a fee for appraising your proposed house. You will provide a set of plans to an appraiser who has been appointed by the lender to perform this service. The appraiser will study your plans, make a review of comparable sales in your geographical area, and ascertain a relative value per square foot of property in the same general neighborhood. The appraiser will take that assumed value per square foot and apply it to the total square footage of your proposed structure and establish a value for the home. If there are special features to be included in the home such as marble floors, energy-saving features such as ceiling fans or extra insulation, and higher grade finishes, the appraiser will take such features into account and add a value factor to the value per square foot. The final appraised value of the proposed home will be the combination of these value factors.

Why is this exercise important? Simple. The lender wants to make certain that the loan you are applying for will amount to at least 80% (depending upon the threshold used by the lender) of the appraised value of the completed house. For example, if, based upon the Borrower's/Builder's Estimate of Costs form, you anticipate that the total cost to construct the house will be $120,000, the lender wants to know that the $120,000 represents at least 80% of the actual value of the house as completed. This means that the pre-construction appraisal must conclude a value of at least $150,000. Note that the appraisal includes the value of the lot on which the structure will be built. And that is what the lender is seeking—a total value of lot and house of at least $150,000. But remember from the discussion of equity that the lender will also expect you to have equity in the project of at least $24,000, or 20% of the loan amount.

Construction Insurance

As a self-contractor, the lender will require that you carry certain insurance coverage. Unlike a licensed residential contractor, you probably will not be required to carry builder's risk insurance (although you should check with your lender to confirm whether or not you must have builder's risk coverage), but in order to protect your liability in case of accident on the job, you will be required to carry construction insurance.

Check with a local insurance agency of your choice for information on the best policy to fit your needs. Often insurance companies will issue a policy that will cover the liability of the self-contractor and will automatically convert to a homeowner's policy at the closing of the permanent loan. You will certainly wish to investigate that possibility. The cost of such a policy is paid at the time that it is obtained for construction, and no additional premiums are payable until its due date, one year later. At the closing of the permanent loan, a sufficient pro rata share of the premium will be collected and placed in escrow, with the remainder of the premium being collected, if you so choose, as a part of your monthly payment. When the premium is due, the lender pays the premium from the collected funds in escrow.

Carefully investigate your options regarding construction insurance. There is a wide latitude among insurers regarding policy provisions and the premiums charged for these provisions. During the construction phase, you will wish to have as much liability coverage as possible. That liability might be reduced, if allowed by the insurer, after the closing of the permanent loan. The primary focus of insurance, however, is to protect you from liability during the construction phase of the project.

CONCLUSION

Financing is critical to whether or not you will actually be allowed to serve as a self-contractor. Approaching the lender is probably the first and the last place where that decision will be rendered. If the lender allows you to be your own contractor, then you will be on the road to reaping large savings in the construction of your home. Remember the key to convincing that lender is to *sell yourself*!

5

REGULATORY AGENCIES
Passing Inspections

I was standing in the unfinished family room of my recently completed home discussing a truss repair job with the framing contractor. He made some suggestions about how the problem could be corrected, suggestions that seemed perfectly plausible to me and the average person. But ... "Before any kind of correction should be made," I said, "let's wait for the inspector to look at the problem." The sub's response was less than enthusiastic. However, it turned out that I was right. The inspector looked at the problem, which involved some critical stress points, and stated that the situation could be corrected only by the careful application of several metal plates, applied with a specific number of nails on either side of the plate on each end. What the framing contractor said after the inspector left is not fit to print.

This scene is not at all unusual. The contractors who are responsible for the construction activities on a house really do not lose any love over the inspectors whose job it is to see that the home is constructed according to certain rules. The inspectors are a lot like referees who see to it that the homeowner is protected from unscrupulous companies who do shoddy work.

It is a fact that no residential construction anywhere in the United States is carried out without the approval of certain regulatory agencies. These agencies may be part of a township, county, or city government. But whatever type of governmental subdivision they belong to, they hold powerful influence over the final outcome of the home. In most cases, the regulations governing the building inspection departments of these governmental subdivisions and/or state legislation provide for a person to serve as his own contractor in the case of residential construction. However, it is extremely important to understand the operations of these departments, the roles they play, and how to get along with them with minimal difficulty. This chapter provides an overview of the types of inspections the department will conduct, what might be expected from these inspections, how to prepare for such inspections, and important tips on how to avoid conflict with the inspectors.

INSPECTION DEPARTMENT ORGANIZATION

Since this book is available in most areas of the United States, it certainly cannot speak to the specific inspection requirements of each city, county, or township. These requirements differ not only from state to state but also many times from county to county and city to city.

Each governmental entity in the United States has adopted a standard housing code, such as the codes published by the Southern Building Code Congress International or the Council of American Building Officials. In addition to the standard code adopted by the governmental entity, it may also, from time to time, enact additional regulations that become a part of the housing code for that specific governmental subdivision. The combination of the standard code and the enacted codes is enforced generally by a building inspections department. This is also the department that issues permits for construction.

Inspection departments are typically organized around the types of inspections they are authorized to conduct. For example, inspections are often conducted only on four major systems of the house or less. These systems include framing (which, besides the actual framing components, encompasses footings, foundations, and slabs, where applicable), electrical, plumbing, and mechanical. In the inspection departments of smaller geographical areas or rural areas, the inspectors may be organized as "1 and 2 family dwelling inspectors" and perform all the systems inspections on such dwellings. This type of organization can also be found in a limited number of metropolitan areas.

The alternative organization departments use is called the "trade inspection" organization. If the governmental subdivision (city or county) code requires inspection for all four systems mentioned above, then the department will employ inspectors who are experts in each of these trades. Each inspector is thus responsible only for the inspections within that trade. For example, an inspector with experience in plumbing will inspect only the requirements included in the plumbing code. An inspector with experience as an electrician will inspect only the electrical system of a house. This type of organization is generally more common among larger governmental subdivisions.

With codes constantly changing and new legislation being enacted, inspectors must update their skills through continuing education. While in some cities and counties continuing education is not required, it is always encouraged at least on a voluntary basis. Generally, funds are available through the department to provide for such continuing education. The inspectors' skills may be updated through seminars, college or technical courses, trade courses, or special workshops. Each inspector is often encouraged to attend a continuing education course at least once each year. In this way, inspectors remain up to date on the latest technology and are more effective in the handling of each case.

WHAT IS INSPECTED?

While the standard code as well as the augmented codes differ from state to state, city to city, and county to county, inspections are typically conducted on four major systems of the house. This section will review each system and offer some examples of what is actually inspected. You will find in the Appendix a sample building permit to be posted at the job site. The posting of the building permit is uniformly a requirement of every governmental subdivision issuing such permits. It is these permits, protected from the weather, which are signed after the passage of each inspection. The signatures attest to the fact that the inspection has indeed been conducted, and the house has passed that particular inspection. The examples of the inspections in this section should not be considered an all-inclusive list. They are simply examples.

Framing Inspection

The framing inspection includes concrete pedestals and footings (if the structure is off-grade), footings, foundation, slab (if the structure is on-grade), and the actual skeletal, structural framework of the house. The main concerns of the framing inspection deal with the anchorage items, which are checked carefully. In the case of footings, the inspector will check for the proper size rebar used in the footings as well as the width and depth of the footing trenches. When the block foundation is laid, the fill dirt placed inside the walls, the under-slab plumbing in place, and the reinforcing rods and wire installed, then the inspector will generally come again to make a final check of the foundation and slab portion of the house. At the same time, the plumbing, electrical, and mechanical inspectors will also inspect in cases where plumbing, electrical, and mechanical components are being placed inside the concrete slab. These inspections are conducted at this point since once the slab is poured, such inspections would be impossible to perform.

As construction proceeds, the framing inspector will typically look for damage to structural elements by other parts of the structure. To obtain maximum structural strength, there should be no damaged or cut structural support members. If another element in the construction poses a hazard to the strength of the support members, then the inspector will require modifications. This is especially important among the roofing or truss members and exterior wall intersections where stress points are so prevalent. Proper bracing is required and will be inspected carefully and in detail to maintain the necessary strength for the roof and exterior wall corners.

The framing inspector will also examine elements involved in fire and draft stoppage. The construction should be of such design as to prevent the rapid spread of fire throughout an attic system or throughout the walls. Besides studying the plans before construction, the inspector will check these elements meticulously and require modifications if they are inadequate.

Another element in the framing inspection considered important by inspectors is the nailing schedule. Obviously, it is not possible for the inspector to check every nail that is driven in a house. Such action would require weeks to inspect just the nails. However, the inspector will make random checks on especially important structural members within the framing schedule. Such members include, but are not limited to, the nailing of sheathing to studs, studs to plates, rafters to plates, floor joists to studs, and corner bracing. If these or other members are found to have inadequate nailing, then the inspector will refuse to sign the inspection sheet and will inform you regarding the corrective measures required.

Electrical Inspection

Remember that, in many inspection departments, these inspections will be conducted by trade experts. That is, these people are not just taken off the streets and asked to do a job. They are tested, evaluated, and judged capable before being placed on the inspection force. Thus, when you call for an electrical inspection, you will likely have a master electrician inspecting the work. He will probably have many years of experience in the electrical construction field and will have been proven capable to inspect by evaluation and experience.

Like many of the other systems inspections, the electrical inspection will require more than one visit from the inspector. He will inspect first the electrical components that might have been installed in the slab; later he will inspect the pre-wiring schedule; near the close of construction he will inspect the final wiring to the circuit breakers (connections, etc.).

Among the major considerations in an electrical inspection will be the size of the wire installed and the number of outlets on each circuit. Fires are more likely to result when the wiring of a house is inadequate to support the electrical load factors. Thus, it is important that the proper size wiring be installed in the house. Furthermore, if circuits become overloaded, fire is inevitable. The inspector will check to determine that the house contains the proper number of outlets per circuit and the proper number of circuits for the building.

In addition to these major concerns, the inspector will check for suitable switch and disconnect controls. Box locations are checked and switch schedules are inspected.

Since the standard housing code will likely contain information regarding outlets and fixtures, the inspector will determine whether the house is being built within the guidelines of the code. He will inspect for the required number of outlets as well as fixtures as required by the code and will make suggestions if any discrepancies exist. While VA and FHA do employ their own inspectors, many building inspectors will also indicate whether the electrical system is in compliance with the FHA or VA specifications. Any suggestions a building inspector makes are not final, however. The final determination is made by the inspector employed by FHA or VA.

Many codes dictate the use of GFI's (Ground Fault Interrupters) around water sources. The inspector will check carefully to ensure that there are GFI's on all outside outlets as well as bathroom and kitchen receptacles.

Plumbing Inspection

As with the electrical inspections, the plumbing inspections will also be conducted in multiple phases. The first inspection will include all components to be installed inside the slab. This inspection is obviously conducted prior to pouring the slab. Later inspections will be conducted when the potable water pipes, waste water pipes (sewer lines), and vents are installed. Usually the final plumbing inspection is conducted when the trench for the sewer line is dug, the sewer pipe installed, and the connection made to the septic system or the city's or county's waste water system.

During the plumbing inspections, the inspector will be checking primarily for proper drainage and vent systems. That is, he ensures that the drain pipes have the proper amount of fall from the house to the septic tank or sewer trunk line.

Without adequate fall, the sewage could backflow into the house.

In addition he will check for proper traps where required, so that neither the water system of the house nor the house itself is exposed to any open sewer waste. He will determine the effectiveness of backflow prevention in the potable water system, thus ensuring that the drinking water flows at a proper rate and does not tend to flow back into the house as the system is shut off. And he will also check on the proper height of the vent system to avoid the infiltration of sewer gas into the house and also to provide pressure equalization. Sewer gas, known as methane, can be explosive and deadly. So the plumbing inspector will ensure that the vent system is adequate to vent out all such gases.

Mechanical Inspection

In some locales, this inspection is not a routine part of the inspection program. In fact, it was only initiated in my own area after the construction of my house. Nevertheless, it can be an important element in the inspection process and probably should be included if it is not already included in all inspection programs.

The major concern regarding the mechanical or HVAC system is to ensure that it doesn't pose a threat to the homeowner. If the system is total electric, the mechanical inspector, along with the electrical inspector, will check for proper wiring, adequate sizing, and sufficient vent system. If the system uses natural or bottled gas, then additional elements require inspection.

In the case of a gas system, the inspector will ensure that the system meets combustion requirements as set forth in the code and will make certain that vent system requirements are also met. These requirements are important to avoid getting inside combustion air rather than outside air. If a system is improperly vented, the combustion chamber of the system will tend to draw inside air from the house in order to achieve the necessary combustion function. If the inside air is used, the oxygen inside the house is soon depleted, thus threatening the lives of the occupants. So the inspector will make sure that the system is properly vented to bring in outside combustion air.

He will also check that the piping has the appropriate cutoff valves. If a gas line into the house has inadequate cutoff valves, then in the case of shutdown, the gas would continue to flow, posing an explosive hazard for the house. So the inspector will check to determine that adequate and proper cutoff valves have been installed.

In any HVAC system, its effectiveness is, in many ways, determined by the adequate flow of air to the various rooms of the house. For example, if a bedroom is 15 X 20 feet and has only one air duct located in it, the room will probably not be adequately heated and cooled. The exact determination of the air moving efficiency is based on the FPM (feet per minute) of air movement. Nevertheless, it is likely that one duct would be inadequate. So the inspector will check the plans and decide conclusively whether the duct system is properly sized, installed, and designed.

Final Inspection

The *final* inspection governs whether the house is ready for occupancy. The components inspected are primarily safety items. Some of the components encompass construction items such as rodent-proof closures, installation of handrails and guardrails, the safe installation of vents over the range hood and in the bathroom, the height of fireplace trim, and the meeting of egress requirements from bedrooms. Once this final inspection is complete and approved, the Certificate of Occupancy can then be issued.

GET READY . . .

I'm not sure that it is possible to prepare for the visit of an inspector, nor is it necessary to pre-

pare beyond having performed the required work. When the work has been completed and prepared for the inspector to evaluate, you are ready to make that all-important call. Some tips on preparing for an inspection might be helpful.

Get to know the inspectors personally. Before you construct your home, call the building inspector's office and arrange a meeting with the inspectors. Learn their names so that when you call for an inspection, you can ask for a specific inspector *by name*. While you may not always get the inspector you request, you usually will, especially if you talk directly with that inspector when you call for the inspection.

Make the call for the inspection in sufficient time to avoid any undue delay. It is highly unlikely that the inspector will be on your job within a short period of time. Remember that he has other jobs to inspect, and he may even be overworked, if you are in an area of rapid growth. It is usually best to call in the early morning for a late morning or early afternoon inspection. His arrival time will depend entirely upon his workload for the day.

Don't estimate completion times. While it is not necessary that the component to be inspected be fully complete at the time of calling for the inspection, make certain that the job will be complete prior to the inspector's arrival. Be absolutely confident that no unforeseen "snags" will be encountered. If the inspector comes to the job site only to find that you called him prematurely, he will be angry, frustrated, and will, in all likelihood, not be prompt for his next inspection.

Ask the subcontractor to remain close by when the inspector arrives. If there is a problem with the inspection, then the subcontractor may be able to convince the inspector that the job was performed properly. If he cannot convince the inspector of a suitable and legal installation, then by being nearby, the inspector will not be constrained to return to his office and make calls to your construction manager or to you in order to explain the problem. If the subcontractor is on site at the time of the inspection, it usually is more smoothly achieved.

Post your house plans. Most codes do not require the on-site posting of plans for residential construction. And while this is not required, I recommend that it be done anyway for the sake of convenience. It is as simple as placing a 3-inch PVC tube, approximately 36 inches long, on the same post as the building permit. By putting end caps on the pipe, a set of plans can be stored in the tube, kept dry, and made available to the building inspectors, if needed. But remember, plans can be changed. The inspectors are dealing with codes, not plans. So long as the changes are within the requirements of the code, then changes are allowed. Nevertheless, it is helpful to have a clean set of plans on site at all times, whether for the inspectors, subcontractors who may have forgotten their plans and left them at home, or others who might be interested in seeing the floor plan of the house.

HERE HE COMES!

I can hear that subcontractor now, "Here he comes, ready to turn us down on everything." But the fact is, such is not really the case. Most inspectors have a job to do, and while contractors and subcontractors view them with suspicion and even disdain at times, the feelings usually are unfounded. That is not to say that you won't sometimes find an inspector with an authority complex, but it does mean that the vast majority of the inspectors realize that they are there only to do the best job possible.

Several tips were mentioned above regarding how to prepare for the visit of an inspector. Here are some tips on how to avoid conflict with an inspector once he arrives on the job site. These may be helpful to you as you begin considering your own construction project.

Be friendly. If you have done your homework, you have already met the person and established a rapport with him. If not, then take the first visit to get acquainted and establish friendly rapport. Act as though your only concern is the soundness of the construction, and you hope that he will assist in every way possible to ensure that soundness. If he is amenable, some small talk—the weather, affairs of the day—can lighten the atmosphere. And then leave the inspector to the work to be inspected.

Ask him if he would like to have you accompany him on the inspection tour. Sometimes the inspector will prefer that you accompany him. When such is the case, ask the inspector if the construction manager may also accompany him. At other times he may prefer to inspect the work and review the results with you, the construction manager, and the subcontractor after the inspection.

Generally, do not have the subcontractor whose work is being checked accompany the inspector unless he (the inspector) specifically requests that the subcontractor accompany him. The inspector can review the work with the subcontractor after the inspection has been completed.

Be flexible but firm. You may recall that earlier, with regard to subcontractors and materials suppliers, you were advised to be firm but flexible. Well, in connection with inspectors, it is the other way around. You need to be flexible but firm. If you are aware that the inspector is requiring you to perform a task that is not required by the code, then you should be firm enough to show him, in a respectful manner, the error of his ways. However, be sure that you know what you are talking about before confronting the inspector with an error.

Most inspectors are willing to listen to an argument on anything that does not relate to the code or laws pertaining to construction. If they are wrong in these non-code-related or non-legal matters, most times they will admit the error and have you proceed without delay. However, if the matter is a subject of the code or law, then the inspector will listen to no argument. You will only build a barrier between you and the inspector if you insist on arguing over a matter of code or law.

Do not be antagonistic. A self-contractor with a chip on his shoulder is inviting trouble with the inspectors. And in conversations with inspectors regarding this type of activity, all unanimously echo, "I will straighten out a contractor who is negative and antagonistic to me. He can either work with me, or I can make it difficult for him." So it is wise to present a positive, friendly, cooperative front to the inspector when he arrives.

Do not allow workers for subcontractors to converse with an inspector unless the situation calls for such conversation. For example, when I experienced the problem with the scissor trusses in the den portion of my house, the inspector stood on the floor and advised the worker how the nailing schedule should be performed. Not only was the inspector present, but also the subcontractor, the self-contractor, and the construction manager. The worker did not argue; he simply proceeded to do what was expected. The inspector passed the work on the first inspection and the job proceeded smoothly. After the inspector left the job site, the subcontractor and the worker mentioned how "ridiculous" the demands were. Nevertheless, the problem had occurred at a critical pressure point on the heavily loaded scissor trusses. As the homeowner as well as the self-contractor, I was pleased that he was so demanding in his inspection. I certainly

do not worry about those trusses falling apart.

As the inspector leaves the job site, be sure to thank him. Thank him for his promptness; thank him for his cooperation; thank him for checking so carefully. Be kind and considerate and remind him that you will be calling again soon for another inspection.

Do not make any kind of offer to the inspector that might be construed as a bribe. While there are probably some inspectors who would accept and might even encourage such offers, you should not make any kind of gesture that might be viewed as a bribe. You do not want to convey that kind of message.

CONCLUSION

Inspectors are very important to the overall construction project. They are there to protect the health and well-being of the homeowner. If they do not perform their duties properly, the health and well-being of the homeowner, and in this case, the self-contractor, are in jeopardy. Do not view inspectors as ogres or trolls whose sole responsibility is to make it difficult for you to construct your home. In most instances, such is not the case. But *do* allow them to do their jobs. This means that, if your construction project is not in keeping with the current codes in force, accept that fact and proceed to make the corrections without complaint. Remember, the future may reveal that inspectors are the reason your life is saved in the case of a disaster.

6

NEGOTIATING ON BUILDING MATERIALS
Getting the Best Deal

Two major factors are involved in the construction of a house. One of these factors will be discussed in the next chapter on subcontractors. The other factor is building materials. No one has yet discovered a way to build a house without materials, and materials cost money.

Probably near the top of the list of expenses incurred in connection with home construction will be the building materials themselves. However, it is certainly not necessary to pay a premium price for such materials. This chapter outlines a strategy for seeking and finding the best prices, negotiating prices and terms with suppliers of building materials, deliveries, COD orders, advantages and disadvantages of certain payment schedules (e.g., COD vs. net or discount terms), and what might be expected, in terms of negotiating strategy, from the various types of suppliers.

BUILDING MATERIALS COMPANIES

Unlike other aspects of the building process, few people have difficulty knowing where to find information about building materials. From the Yellow Pages of the phone book to the Sunday supplements in the newspaper, there exists an abundance of information on sources of building materials. Building materials, in the context of this chapter, will also refer to supplies such as fixtures, flooring, and the like.

Types of Building Supply Companies

There are almost as many types of building supply companies as there are types of building supplies. There are major suppliers of building materials who carry an extensive line of materials rather than what might be called specialty materials. Such large suppliers may carry lumber, hardware supplies such as nails, screws, bolts, wire, and so forth. There are even building materials companies where you could, conceivably, purchase all your building materials from the batter boards to the carpeting.

In addition to the general building supply sources, there usually are businesses that supply limited kinds of building materials.

Sawmills and wholesale lumber mills—Instead of purchasing the lumber from a large building supply company in your city, it may be possible to purchase the lumber to be used in your home directly from the "factory" or sawmill if you are in an area where the sawmills operate. Doing this may avoid the "middle men" who place their own profits on top of the cost of the lumber from the mill. This is a source of excellent potential savings.

Concrete supply companies—These companies —and there are probably several in your city—can provide the concrete to be used in the footings, foundation, slab, and other areas of the proposed house.

Brick/masonry companies — Brick yards are plentiful in most cities of any size. These companies can supply brick and mortar as well as other supplies, such as lintels, which the brick mason will require. There may be instances when the brick company will not carry concrete block, or what has been known in the past as "cinder block." If the brick company does not carry a line of concrete block, it will be necessary to find a maker of these materials, if you plan to use them.

Sand companies—Sand will be needed as the stabilizer for cement used in laying brick or concrete block. Further, fill dirt will be needed if you plan to build a house on grade—which means that a concrete slab will be poured rather than having the house built on concrete pylons.

Insulation companies — These firms provide lines of insulation for both walls and ceilings. Other insulation-type materials such as foam filler may also be used and can be obtained from these sources.

Electrical supply companies—If your electrical subcontractor does not supply the materials for wiring the house, you may wish to investigate the suppliers of electrical wire, panels, boxes, face plates, plugs, switches, and so forth.

Lighting fixture companies—Often the lighting fixtures can be purchased from the same source as the electrical supply materials.

Appliances — Careful investigation will show that appliances can be bought from companies that regularly do business with contractors. Even major chains like Sears can provide appliance packages for your house.

Ceiling fans — While you probably would be able to obtain ceiling fans from either the electrical supply company or the lighting fixture company, there are also firms whose sole business is the sale of ceiling fans and accessories.

Drywall supply companies—These companies can supply the gypsum board and all the supplies necessary to finish it. These companies may also carry lines of other supplies such as roof vents, fireplaces, or insulation.

Site preparation companies—You will probably need to have your home site prepared before actual construction can begin. It will require clearing and grading, removal of tree stumps and debris, and leveling. Landscape companies or heavy equipment operators are typically in the business to do this part of the job for you.

Window companies—These are generally suppliers of sash windows; however, specialty window companies have sprung up in the last few years. So if your plans call for specialty windows such as semi-circles, quarter-circles, or non-standard size windows, those may ordered from companies that provide custom window services.

Door companies—These companies should be able to provide doors for both the exterior and interior of the house. Such companies may carry lines of door handles, locks, and hinges; or it may be necessary to obtain the handles, locks, and hinges from another source.

Truss companies—Trusses are usually the least expensive means of constructing roofs on most structures. Therefore, if the roof of your house is not to be hand-framed, then you will wish to contact a truss company for the purchase of the truss system.

HOW TO BEGIN

To begin the process of ordering materials, you must have some idea as to the quantities you will need of various types of materials. For example, how many 8-foot wall studs will you actually need? How many 2 X 12's will be required? How many sheets of oxboard will be needed for the upstairs flooring? How many sheets of plywood will be needed for the roof?

Since you will not be an expert in calculating these quantities, how can you possibly know how much of what needs to be ordered? Well, here's the answer. Go to the Yellow Pages of your telephone book and turn to the section headed "Building Materials." Search there for one or two large, diversified building materials suppliers who are well-known in your city. Call these companies and ask to speak to the "estimator." Many of these companies have personnel who specialize in estimating the materials requirements for a job. When the estimator answers, inform him that you are in the early stages of building a home as a self-contractor, and you are looking for the best materials package that you can find at the most reasonable cost. Ask him if his company would be interested in providing an estimate of the "basic materials package" for your house. The likely answer will be "yes." When that has been determined, take a set of the construction documents to the estimator of the two suppliers and have them perform a detailed estimate of each major construction component in the house. These would primarily include: (1) footings, (2) slab (if a slab is to be included), (3) first floor framing package (if more than one floor), (4) second floor framing package (if second floor is included), (5) decking and sheathing, (6) exterior doors, (7) windows, (8) siding and cornices, (9) roof, (10) brick (if used), (11) drywall, and (12) interior trim.

On these components, ask for an estimate sheet listing the quantity, description of the material, the unit price, and the total price of each unit of material. (See Appendix for Sales Estimate of Major Components.) The building materials company will be happy to provide this estimate for you. And remember, you are not obligated to purchase your materials from the company providing the estimate.

I recommend that this estimate be obtained from two different suppliers of building materials. You will likely order some of your materials from these suppliers, but you certainly are not obligated to do so. Nevertheless, the exercise will be of immeasurable assistance to you when you begin to order the framing package and other materials for the construction. Also, in order to arrive at a reasonably accurate estimate of the cost of the major construction components, add the total of each of the components listed.

FINDING BUILDING MATERIALS SUPPLIERS

With regard to the construction of a house, the most common question always relates to "finding" something—either materials or subcontractors. Finding building materials is probably the easiest part of this question to answer since most people know that the phone book is a logical source of such information.

Before embarking on a search for building materials suppliers, it is wise, if possible, to meet with a contractor friend or a person who has built a house recently, either one of whom can enlighten you as to the best sources of building materials, and especially the quality of such building materials. When you meet with these people, you should take notes you can later transfer to the Building Materials Suppliers form in the Appendix. This form will help you maintain a record of the materials you order and from whom you order them.

Using the information gathered in these conversations, arm yourself with the telephone book and begin a thorough search of the various headings advertising materials suppliers. By this point you will have already identified at least two major, diversified suppliers of building materials. And you will have secured from them an estimate of the quantities needed for the major components in the job.

As you begin this search, make sure that you have several copies of the Building Materials Suppliers form. You will need at least one for each construction component. That is, you will need one for the framing package, one for the brick supplier, one for the wallboard supplier, one for the windows, etc. While you will certainly search in specialty categories for building suppliers, for example, "Carpet & Rug Dealers — New," you will also wish to search in the section headed "Building Materials — Retail." These companies are typically large, sometimes discount-type operations, which market a wide range of building supplies. In fact, it is not uncommon to be able to purchase almost an entire construction package from such a supplier. Examples of these suppliers might be chain operations like Lowe's, Scotties, and Wickes Lumber, or a locally-owned building supply company. You will need a copy of the General Suppliers form (see Appendix) for each large supply company. It is divided into different materials categories and provides space to include unit costs of various types of building materials. Be sure to have the General Suppliers form and the Building Materials Suppliers form validated by authorized signature.

One important source you should not overlook in the process of finding and negotiating for building materials is the special inserts in your daily newspaper. Many of these inserts are printed by building supply companies and provide information on the "specials" that are being offered. These specials are generally offered for a limited time but may offer considerable savings over the negotiated prices of other companies. Keep a careful eye on these inserts and make notes of the prices on all the items to be used in constructing your house, comparing them with the items on your Suppliers forms. When these specials appear, check them out carefully, and if

they are of equal quality to the materials previously selected, then take advantage of them. If the materials being offered on special are not needed at the present time, take advantage of the specials anyway and stockpile the materials for later use on the job site.

NEGOTIATING PRICES AND TERMS

Once you have identified the suppliers you plan to contact for prices, the enjoyable part begins—negotiating the pricing structure of the various component parts. Note that some of the suppliers will have a greater latitude in pricing than other suppliers; that is, the salespeople or company manager can reduce the prices without prior approval from a home office or higher officer. In the case of locally-owned businesses, the owner may be on duty and can authorize reductions in prices. In this case you will wish to negotiate directly with the owner.

The negotiating strategy that you will employ will depend in large measure upon the type of supplier you are negotiating with. For example, if you are seeking the lowest possible cost for a framing package, it is probably better that you purchase the entire package from one supplier rather than studs from one supplier, joists from another, and 12-foot 2 X 4's from yet another. The supplier of lumber for a framing package can lower prices on certain items while maintaining a regular price on others, thereby offering you a compromise package price. In the long run, this will be to your advantage. On the other hand, when dealing with a brick supplier, the ability of the supplier to reduce the price is quite limited. You might get the supplier to lower his price per thousand by 1 to 2%, or he may offer you the regular firm price with a 1 to 2% discount for cash payment within ten days of shipment to the job site. The important point is that certain suppliers can offer attractive discounts while others may not.

When negotiating prices, do not be shy. When a price has been quoted to you, be aggressive and ask the salesperson if an additional "X" percent or if "Y" dollars or cents couldn't be taken off the price. You will be surprised how often the price will be reduced, even if not by as much as requested.

And do not be reluctant to play one supplier against another, especially in geographical areas where construction has been on a decline. After you have obtained quotes on supplies and have these quotes on your form, review the form and determine whether there might be, among the suppliers, those who might need the business enough to reduce their price to that of a competitor who quoted a lower price. Call that supplier and say: "ABC quoted me _____ on the shingles per square. Your price is $_____ above that price. Since your price is more competitive on the felt for the roof, I would really like to get all the roofing materials from you. Would you be willing to lower your price to that of ABC? If so, I will get all my roofing materials from you rather than from ABC. However, if you can't meet their price, I will just split the purchase orders." You will be surprised at how fast the company may lower the price just to get all your roofing business.

Negotiation is really a matter of "reading" those with whom you negotiate. All people give off information that indicates a willingness or non-willingness to negotiate. Be cognizant of these signs. Some of the signs are:

Body language — The way a person squirms, drums his fingers, shifts his eyes, scribbles on paper, appears nervous, or moves about in his chair are all evidence of negotiability. Note especially eye contact or the lack thereof. These actions convey a lack of confidence in one's position and can be signs that negotiation is probable in this situation.

Defensive/argumentative — Salespeople who want your business but are afraid that they will not get it often become defensive and argumentative. They attempt to exhibit confidence but generally demonstrate, by their actions and words, that they are quite unsure of their position relative to their competition. Or you may hear them say: "You can bet you won't find this item less anywhere else in town." Chances are, you will, if you look long enough.

Key words — Listen for important words and phrases that often indicate a willingness to negotiate. Among those key words or phrases would be "well," "we might be able to help you," "I guess," "chances are," and "check around." This list is certainly not all-inclusive but provides an insight into the kind of listening that you as a self-contractor should do. The phrases indicate hesitancy on the part of the salesperson—a hesitancy about the firmness of his pricing schedule. Often he is willing to negotiate when he is unsure of his position relative to the competition.

Yet another consideration that can lead to significant savings is to be sure to ask about discounts on demonstrator items. Of course, this tactic will not be effective in the case of lumber or brick but, for example, when shopping for plumbing fixtures such as bathtubs, toilets, kitchen sinks, and the like, be sure to ask whether the supplier has any demonstrator models that might be available for purchase. Often, these models, especially if purchased immediately after a home show, can be bought for 25 to 50% below regular price.

When negotiating on items in this manner, be sure to inspect the product before you take final possession of it. In most cases, suppliers will not attempt to offer broken or defective materials to you; however, you must take care to inspect every inch of the item being purchased to ensure against defect. Once the item has been delivered at the price quoted, generally, the supplier will not accept it as a return item, even if it is found to be defective. This is probably the best example of *caveat emptor*, "let the buyer beware," of which I have personal knowledge. Yet purchasing fixtures and similar supplies in this manner can provide excellent savings opportunities.

Negotiating prices is an art. The attitude with which you, the self-contractor, enter the negotiations can, in many cases, have a profound influence upon the outcome. For example, if you go into negotiations with the idea that you will win at all costs, then your strategy is flawed, and you will not realize the savings you might otherwise have realized. Let me share some attitudinal approaches that are important for you to possess as you enter negotiation on building supplies.

1. Recognize the need for the supplier to earn a profit. While it is important that the supplier earn a profit, the size of that profit is the negotiable part. To earn a profit of 100% is one position the supplier might have, but to earn a profit of 20% is another. Your responsibility is to allow the supplier to make a reasonable profit without gouging you. And not only should you recognize his right to the profit, but you should also acknowledge that right in his presence. If the supplier sees that you are reasonable in your expectations, he will likely be more cooperative in his pricing structure.

2. Enter negotiations with a cooperative spirit. Do not enter the process with an attitude of spitefulness, nor should you develop such an attitude during the course of the process. So be firm in your position, but be willing to "give" when reasonable times for "giving" present themselves. Do not try to get back at a supplier for a previous action. This kind of attitude will likely backfire.

3. Be kind and respectful. Recognize that the other person is only doing his job. You should treat him with the same kindness, respect, and dignity with which you expect to be treated. He deserves it.

4. Be considerate. Do not take issue with the salesman personally. Nothing that he says or does is directed at you personally, so you should respect that position and treat him in the same manner. Do not issue personal attacks at him simply because he is unwilling to bend to your wishes. Rather, treat him with professional dig-

nity. You'll be surprised at how far this attitude will take you in the negotiation process.

5. Smile as much as possible; even be humorous. You will be amazed at how a smile or humor will affect others. Even when the salesman says he can't offer you the discount you want, keep smiling and negotiating. Sometimes all it takes is a little time to pass, and you can get near to or exactly what you seek.

If you are negotiating prices with a supplier of multiple lines of building materials, be keenly aware that you should negotiate as many lines of these building supplies as possible. For example, if you have a supplier of insulation who also sells pre-fab fireplaces, foam, ridge vents, ceiling fans, and attic fans, you should negotiate the prices of all of these items or at least as many of these items as you plan to build into your home. While you may purchase only a few of these items, you will, nevertheless, have the benefit of the total negotiation process to help you in the long run.

When you negotiate prices, be sure to ask about any additional charges. More will be mentioned later about terms, but you must be aware of whether there will be costs such as delivery charges added to the billing statement. In addition, have the contact person with the supplier inform you as to the length of time that the prices are effective. Sometimes companies have a policy that quotations are good for only twenty or thirty days, so if you get a quotation on July 2 and you place the order on August 10, you may pay an updated price. So ask the salesperson or the company manager to put in writing and sign a statement as to the period of time during which the prices quoted are effective.

If, during the course of construction, you find that there are building materials for which you have not received quotations, you may feel free to go first to suppliers you are using and who are most likely to have the materials, to determine whether they might be competitive or not. To cross-check, you simply might make phone calls to two or three other suppliers to determine the first supplier's competitive positions. But whoever you decide to use, get, in writing, the effective period of the prices.

Finally, be aware that you cannot expect to get supplies at the same prices as the licensed contractors of your area. You ask, "Why?" Simple. The suppliers are aware that you are building only one house. The likelihood of getting additional business from you is lessened by the fact that you are a self-contractor building one home. The licensed residential contractors may construct ten, twenty, or more homes a year. Therefore, the suppliers recognize the high possibility of future business if they are competitive. So negotiate your best price, with the understanding that you will not be able to meet the pricing structure offered to the licensed residential contractors.

HOW BUILDING MATERIALS ARE SOLD

Take this example: Ron goes to the major supplier of building materials and says, "I want to buy 150 8-foot 2 X 4 wall studs. Can you tell me the price per board foot?" Or he may go to the brick company and ask, "Can you give me the price per hundred on 25,000 brick?" The answer to these questions most assuredly would be "yes," but the prices are being requested in increments that are not customary. So how do we purchase supplies? The following list, while not all-inclusive, will provide a review of the increments in which major component materials are sold.

Lumber—Lumber is typically purchased by the building materials company by the board foot. And at times, it will be sold to you by the board foot. However, since most modern houses are framed in materials that are often of standard lengths, the materials are generally available by the piece. For example, you would order 2 X 4 studs in standard 8-foot lengths and purchase them by the piece. If the purchase of 2 X 4 studs

is to be made in non-standard lengths, for example, 9-foot lengths, then the supplier may wish to sell the lumber to you by the board foot rather than by the piece. In order to indicate your knowledge of the business, you might ask whether the studs would be purchased by the board foot or by the piece.

Other lumber, that is, 2 X 6, 2 X 12, 2 X 14, and other types of lumber included in the framing package, are generally purchased by the piece. Plywood or oxboard, Styrofoam® sheathing, Thermoply®, sound board, rebar, etc. are all sold by the piece. And the more pieces that are to be purchased, the greater the price break that can be offered. In all of these cases, the salesman will give you a "unit price" which informs you of the price per piece. If the unit price is $7.95 and you expect to purchase fifty units or pieces, then the price is $7.95 times 50 or $397.50. These prices do not include tax or a delivery charge, if applicable.

Brick/Stone—Brick is sold by the thousand or fractions thereof. For example, if the price of the brick is $165 per thousand and you purchase 10,000 brick for your home, the price is calculated to be $165 times ten. If you planned to purchase 10,500 brick for your house, then the price would be $165 times 10.5.

Concrete blocks and stone are priced differently. These materials are typically sold by the piece. Concrete blocks are manufactured in several different forms, and each form has a different pricing structure.

Roofing materials — For the new home, two major components comprise the roofing materials — felt (tarpaper) and shingles. The felt is a black composite paper substance used to provide a barrier between the wood of the roof decking and the shingles that form the outer covering. It is produced and sold by the roll, usually 50 feet, and by weight. That is, the standard residential roof would use 15-pound roofing felt. The number of rolls needed would be determined by the roof area to be covered. One roll should cover approximately one square.

Shingles are sold by the square. A square is an area of 100 square feet. Shingles are sold in asphalt or fiberglass forms. Specific warranties on the types of shingles should be discussed with the supplier.

Vinyl siding—While your subcontractor may be able to get the materials for prices less than you could purchase them, you must be aware that siding is purchased in squares, much like roofing shingles. In fact, your sub will probably give you a quotation based on the "number of squares" of siding to be installed.

Tile/ceramics — These materials may be purchased by the piece or more often than not may be sold by the square foot. However, when comparing prices, be sure to keep the unit prices parallel so that you are not comparing materials sold by the square foot by one supplier with those sold by the piece by another supplier.

Guttering—The installer will generally prefer to obtain his own materials in the case of the installation of gutters and downspouts. This may also be a better and less expensive approach for you.

Plumbing supplies — This category includes a wide variety of materials. The primary material to be used is piping. Whether PVC or metal piping materials are used, they are almost always sold by the foot. "T's," joints, elbows, and the like are then sold by the piece. As with some of the other subsystems in the house, the materials for this system may better be provided by the subcontractor. Negotiate the materials with the price of the labor if possible. You will probably incur less expense.

Electrical supplies — As with the plumbing supplies, there is a variety of materials to be used in the electrical system of the home. Wiring is generally sold in boxes of a specific length, and these boxes cannot be broken. Most other supplies are purchased by the piece. However, you may again

be in a better position if you negotiate both materials and labor with the electrical subcontractors.

Concrete — Always sold by the cubic yard. The prices vary and can be negotiated, but the price will always be based upon the number of cubic yards or fractions thereof delivered to the job site.

If you are ever in doubt as to the increments in which materials are sold, remember that you can review the building supplies estimate, which you will have already obtained from a major general building supply dealer. This estimate will list the units in which the supplies and materials are obtainable. Or, in the absence of such an estimate, don't be afraid to ask the salesman about the increments or units in which the supplies or materials are sold. He will not think less of you, and your asking will not affect the pricing structure he will provide.

CHOOSING YOUR MATERIALS SUPPLIERS

After you have conducted the necessary research, and after you have spent considerable time negotiating prices, it is time to determine the supply companies you plan to use. Using the Suppliers to be Used form, place the name of the company, the contact person, the phone number, the terms of payment negotiated, effective period of prices, and the prices of materials as indicated. Use the "Notes" section for information such as delivery schedules and any other miscellaneous notices. You will need to use one form for each of the following recommended categories:

Concrete	Windows
Foundation Materials	Carpeting/Flooring
Site Preparation	Glazed Tile
Roofing	Plumbing
Framing Package	Electrical
Brick/Masonry	HVAC
Insulation	Fixtures
Drywall/Gyp Board	Paint/Wallpaper
Doors	Lighting

Once these forms have been completed, keep them together for quick and ready reference. You may need to use them to check on prices of other minor materials as the need for such materials arises.

DELIVERIES

Just think how difficult it would be if you had to go to the suppliers each day and get the materials to be used on the job for that day. You would need a special flatbed truck with sufficient length to carry 14- and 16-foot pieces of lumber, sides high enough to carry the materials adequately stacked, and a means of unloading that would not break your back.

Well, much to your advantage, most suppliers *do* make deliveries. When you place an order for supplies, the salesperson will ask you when you want the materials delivered. Therefore, make sure that when you place the order you have in mind a time you want the materials to be delivered. When asked, inform the salesperson of that time. The requested time is placed on order forms, and every effort is made by the supplier to meet that deadline for delivery.

It is important that you place the order far enough in advance to ensure the timely delivery of the materials. Many suppliers cannot operate on short notice. In fact, when you determine the suppliers of your materials and so inform them, be sure to inquire as to the amount of advance notice they require in order to make timely deliveries. Place this delivery information on the Suppliers to be Used form in the "Notes" section. While most companies cannot operate on short notice, you might be surprised to know that there are companies that can make deliveries on quite short notice.

Deliveries are an important part of the construction process. If you do not place orders in sufficient time to have deliveries made when the materials are needed, you may find a subcontractor idle, waiting for materials to be delivered. And you will find that an idle subcontractor will generally not stay idle for very long. He will go to another job, thereby losing a day's work on your construction project. Therefore, be keenly aware of the advance notice required by suppliers for delivery of materials.

PAYMENT FOR MATERIALS

Essentially there are three ways to pay for the materials used in your home construction project. However, not all supply companies will have the three payment plans available to you. Because you are a one-time purchaser, the supplier will likely inform you as to which payment schedules will be available. Nevertheless, my best advice to you with regard to payment of bills, regardless of the payment plan used, is to use an existing checking account or establish a separate checking account for the purpose of writing checks as payment for these bills. After all, cancelled checks are the best receipt for paid statements. *Never pay a materials supplier in cash!*

Cash on Delivery

The first of these payment schedules is "COD," Cash on Delivery. It is the most common means of payment and is most likely to be the one required by your suppliers. It means simply that, when the delivery is made to your job site, the delivery person will have in his possession a billing statement or invoice with the amount owed. The company will expect that delivery person to return to the company with a check or cash in the amount of the billing statement or invoice. If you refuse to pay the delivery person, the materials will not be unloaded at your job site but returned to the company location.

But what if there is a mistake in the billing statement? That is a good question! And there are two possible answers. The first, and most usable, is to go to a telephone and call the contact person on your Suppliers to be Used form. Inform him that the billing statement is in error and what the error is, as you perceive it. Ask him to get a copy of the billing statement and review it with you while you are on the phone. If, indeed, the statement is in error, then get the delivery person to talk with the salesman or contact person to obtain an authorization to complete the delivery on payment of the amount you and the contact person have agreed upon. Pay that amount, the delivery is made, and the transaction concluded. Be sure, however, to note on the statement the changes authorized by the contact person, the time of day, the date, and the signature of the driver acknowledging that the payment was, in fact, made to him. You then have written evidence of the transaction.

But what if you and the contact person cannot arrive at an agreement as to the amount owed? In order to avoid a delay in the construction process, proceed by writing a check in the amount of the billing statement or invoice, but at the same time, inform the contact person that you will be in his office personally to resolve the issue. As soon as possible after the delivery, proceed to the office of the supplier and resolve the matter. If the matter is resolved in your favor, the company will be happy to provide a refund or a credit on future purchases. If the matter is not resolved in your favor, then the transaction stands. If you are dissatisfied with the transaction, you may wish to check on your second priority supplier for future business in that category.

Net/Discount Terms

The second type of payment schedule is "net/discount terms." What this plan allows is for a discount to be issued in the case of "prompt" payment. This is not a charge account but does allow the self-contractor a few days "float time" to make payment without having to keep the checkbook at the job site constantly. Typically, under this plan, materials are delivered, and the purchaser has ten days to pay the bill in order to realize a specified discount, usually 1 to 2%. If

paid after that date, the full bill, or net amount, is due and payable. This is an excellent plan which allows some flexibility in payment yet provides a discount as an incentive for prompt payment.

Charge Account

The third type of payment schedule is a charge account. Like any other charge account, under this type schedule, the supplier delivers the materials or supplies to the job site, requires an authorized signature on a delivery voucher acknowledging receipt of the materials, and allows the self-contractor to pay for the supplies only after receipt of a billing statement, usually thirty days later or at the end of the month. The delivery voucher will contain the types and number of units of each material delivered. This delivery voucher should be kept as a cross-check with the billing statement when it is received. The receipt of the billing statement obviously is dependent upon the time of the month in which the billing statements are mailed versus the time of the month on which the delivery is made. No discounts are permitted under this plan, and the billing statement can, and often does, reflect the bills from several deliveries.

While the charge account is very convenient to the self-contractor, many suppliers are reluctant to provide that service. To get a charge account, you must apply for it as with any other retail establishment, having your references and credit checked. However, the convenience of the billing process sometimes will offset the inconvenience of having to go through the application process. When the billing statements are received, you should carefully review them for correct pricing and correct delivery amounts. These amounts will appear on the delivery voucher you or another authorized person signed. Make sure that the delivered units on the voucher match correctly the amounts shown on the billing statement. If there is a discrepancy of any kind—either in the unit pricing or units delivered—call your contact person for resolution of the matter.

CONCLUSION

Researching and negotiating on building materials can be one of the most time-consuming exercises in which you will engage as a self-contractor. The savings can be quite significant, however, if properly and vigorously pursued. After all, building materials form a large part of the construction requirements for the house. But remember to be relentless in your pursuit of the best deals, and be firm in your negotiation. While you will not want to be abusive, be sufficiently confident that the salesman will want to do business with you. In the final analysis *you* will be the winner.

7

ENLISTING SUBCONTRACTORS
Finding and Contracting

As was mentioned in Chapter 6, one of the two major factors in home construction is enlisting subcontractors. Inevitably, the question most often posed to me regarding self-contracting is: How did you find your subcontractors to do the work? And while this is an important question, it appears to be the most bothersome concern of potential self-contractors.

But there definitely is a secret to this part of the plan. This chapter outlines at least six ways in which subcontractors can be identified, contacted, and enlisted. Furthermore, you will be shown how to determine the quality of each subcontractor's work so that you can eliminate any whose work quality is below that which you desire.

After identifying the subcontractors for the specific type of work, negotiation regarding cost can be initiated. There is considerable room for negotiation on almost every element of the construction plan. This chapter provides a step-by-step plan for negotiating with subcontractors.

This chapter will also inform you of what you might expect from subcontractors. Almost without exception, subcontractors comprise a subculture with its own identity. They are unique in

the ways in which they operate, and working with them can often be frustrating. This chapter deals with working with subcontractors, how and when to pay them, and ways to protect yourself from unscrupulous operators who sometimes prey on the unsuspecting.

KNOWING THE SUBCONTRACTOR COMPONENTS

Before you search for or enlist subcontractors, it would be wise to know the types of subcontractors you need to enlist. It really is easy, since all you must do is look at the various components of the house. Each component will reveal the kind of subcontractor required.

For example, if the house is to be constructed with a slab on grade, that is, a solid one-piece concrete slab poured directly on the ground, you will need to enlist a subcontractor to lay out the foundation of the house and pour and finish the slab. Therefore, a subcontractor who sets batter boards, digs for footings, and finishes slabs will be required to perform this task. Typically, a concrete finisher will perform all of these duties mentioned and will also lay concrete block for the foundation of the house. It is necessary to find this subcontractor early since he is generally the one who begins work on the house once the lot has been cleared, graded, and leveled.

In addition to this subcontractor, other subcontractors will be needed to complete the house. The following list will explain who they are but, because the construction phasing of each house is different, the list is not in any particular order. However, all the contractors should be enlisted prior to or in the very early stages of construction, so that no time is lost in the construction phase because of the non-enlistment of a subcontractor.

Lot preparation—To construct a home, the lot must be cleared of all vegetation and other obstructions. This work is often performed by land clearing companies whose sole business is the preparation of construction sites. Additional services such as digging ponds and lakes, bush hogging, and back filling are often offered by these companies.

Another type of company that can perform this kind of service includes landscape contractors or other lawn and garden businesses that provide landscaping services. Such a company will often have grading equipment to remove trees, stumps, and debris from a homesite. You should check with local nurseries or landscaping companies to determine whether they have the capability to clear your lot and level and grade the site.

Yet another option is to enlist the services of a grading contractor or heavy equipment company. With heavy equipment already in inventory to perform such activities, these companies will often take on smaller jobs just to keep the equipment in useful and operating condition. Furthermore, if a piece of equipment is not in use on a particular day, the company will view favorably the prospects of earning additional income with an otherwise idle piece of equipment. Often this results in a bargain for you as well.

Survey company — After the lot has been cleared, graded, and leveled, and the homesite is finally prepared for the actual construction, it is necessary to enlist the services of a survey company. The survey company will perform two very special tasks. The crew will first survey the lot, reconfirming for the mortgage company that the lot actually is as it is described in the mortgage company's paperwork. In addition, the crew will take the plans for the house as drawn by the designer and lay out the four corners and any other special corner notations that might be required by the footings crew. These stake placements will be used as reference points over which to draw strings attached to batter boards. The purpose of this exercise is to determine the precise placement and configuration of the footings to be dug.

Framing subcontractor—After the slab has been poured or, if the structure is to be built off-grade, the pilings have been positioned by the footings and foundation subcontractor, then it is time for the framer to begin his work. The framer's responsibility is to construct all skeletal or structural framework for the house, including the exterior walls and all interior walls. The framer also will frame staircases, windows and doorways, fireplaces (if a prefabricated fireplace will be used), and will place and attach roofing trusses, if trusses are used. If trusses are not used, the framer will be responsible for hand-framing the roofing system. After placement of trusses or hand-framing of the roofing system, the framer also will attach the roof covering, called decking, which will be either marine plywood or oxboard, and cover it with an appropriate grade of black felt material. He is also responsible for the installation of all sub-flooring and exterior insulated coverings such as foam board, Thermoply®, or soundboard.

Once all the skeletal framing is in place, the framer can go back and install the components for which he has provided framing. For instance, the windows will be attached to the frames provided, and the jambs for the exterior doors will be positioned.

Electrical subcontractor — After the house has been framed, it is time to call in the subcontractors whose responsibility includes installation of components inside the walls. Ideally, three subcontractors might be operating at the same time to complete their responsibilities inside the walls. One of these is the electrician. He can install all electrical lines inside the walls as well as the junction boxes, that is, boxes for the switches and receptacles. Since most of his work is inside the walls, the greatest portion of his responsibility will be concluded once he has finished. He needs to return only for the final trim-out of all electrical fixtures near the end of construction.

Plumbing subcontractor — This subcontractor can also be installing components at the same time that the electrician is installing wires, etc. The plumber will have begun his work earlier when he installed lines throughout the fill dirt prior to the pouring of a slab. But at this point in the construction phase, he will install the necessary wall components prior to the covering of the walls.

Heating, ventilation, and air conditioning (HVAC) subcontractor—This subcontractor also can be installing ductwork and vent frames within the walls and ceilings at the same time that the electrician and plumber are installing their wall elements. This subcontractor will also have installed exhaust lines and conduit within the fill dirt prior to the pouring of a slab.

Drywall subcontractor — Once the necessary components have been installed inside the walls, the drywall subcontractor can begin. He is responsible for installing the gypsum board on walls and ceilings, taping and sealing all seams, installing corner beads, and providing the required finishes for both walls and ceilings.

Roofing subcontractor—It is good to know that the high prices you may be familiar with in the roofing business only apply to the reinstallation of roofs. The roofer will install the eave metal on the edges of the eaves and the shingles or other roofing materials required by the design. His installations include all flashing materials around fireplace chimneys and other interrupting surfaces on or about the roof and the installation and sealing of roof vents and ridge vents. The cost of these efforts will probably bring a smile of relief.

Brick subcontractor—If your home is to have exterior walls of brick or a fireplace on the inside, you will need to find a bricklaying company. The brick masons will install brick on the exterior, including steps, trim brick around porches, and brick mailbox stanchions. On the interior, any brick surfaces will be installed by this subcontractor. These surfaces might include a wall behind a stove, a brick fireplace, brick floors, or other such surfaces.

Miscellaneous subcontractors—As you can see from the list, numerous subcontractors are required to complete the construction of a house. For convenience, I am including here a list of required subs, but which I do not number among the major subcontractors. This listing is not intended to downplay their importance, because every element in the construction is equally important. But while their work is probably among the most noticeable as to quality, their relative costs and responsibilities are less than the major subcontractors.

Among these subcontractors I include insulation, tile/ceramics, vinyl (if vinyl is used on any of the exterior of the house), paint, wallpaper, cabinetry, and wood interior trim. Each of these is a subcontract specialty unto itself. You will need to enlist and negotiate with each of these in order to complete the home project.

GETTING THE RIGHT SUBCONTRACTOR FOR THE JOB

One of the most time-consuming activities in which you as a self-contractor will engage is searching for, finding, enlisting, and negotiating with subcontractors. They form a major force in getting the job done and getting it done properly. So you do not want simply to take the first crew that comes along. You will want to do some intensive research before deciding on the specific subcontractor you wish to use on each construction component. I can hear you saying: "But how do I find them?!" Let's see if we can answer that critical question.

Finding the Right Subcontractor

There are at least six ways to search out subcontractors for the job. You may wish to use one or more or all of these procedures in determining the right subcontractor for your job. They are not listed here in priority order but are simply different ways of approaching this problem.

You will want to maintain a list of the potential subcontractors, which you will compile from these various sources. Use the Prospective Subcontractor form (see Appendix) to maintain this list. Once you have negotiated a contract with a particular subcontractor, that sub's name and company information will be transferred to the Project Subcontractors form, also in the Appendix. But let's begin by considering the ways in which subcontractors can be found and enlisted.

Contact other contractors. I can hear you saying, "Why would a licensed contractor give me the names of subcontractors?" The answer really is easy. The licensed contractor knows that you will be building only one house. If you build a beautiful home with subcontractors he uses, he can point to your home as well as ones he has built as an example of the kind and quality of work he constructs, simply because you have used the same subs.

Furthermore, you probably have a friend who is in the construction business. Go to him and be honest with him about your project. Ask him if he will be so kind as to help you identify subcontractors you could use on your job. You will be surprised to find that he will cooperate with

you to the fullest degree. If not, you have lost nothing. Go to a licensed contractor you do not know and follow the same procedure.

How do you select a contractor you do not know? Unless your city is unlike most cities I am familiar with, home contractors have a reputation for building either quality homes or homes of not so good quality. You will want to select a contractor who builds homes of excellent quality, even expensive custom homes.

Once you have selected one or two of these contractors, set up appointments to go and visit with them. When I face a contractor I do not know, I begin by complimenting him or her on the quality of the houses he or she constructs. I mention that I have selected this contractor because of reputation and want to be able to pass that reputation on to others. Then I mention that I am contracting my own home and would like to enlist his help in identifying subcontractors he uses and whom I might contact for use on my construction project.

You may find that the contractor will attempt to talk you out of doing the project on your own. But your best response is to say that the project has proceeded past the point that it can be bid out. After that has been explained to the contractor, he or she will likely cooperate to a surprisingly agreeable point.

When I was beginning the process on my own home, I visited a licensed contractor to obtain the names of potential subs. As mentioned, he asked me if I had ever built a house before, to which I replied, "No." Then he asked me if I was sure that I could carry through on this kind of project with such limited knowledge. I replied that I was confident that I could do so. Then he proceeded to cooperate with me by providing a complete list of names and telephone numbers of potential subcontractors, even to the team that would perform the final cleaning services. So it is possible, if approached appropriately, to have a licensed contractor provide you with the names of potential subcontractors. Place the names and information about these subcontractors on the Prospective Subcontractors form.

Visit other home construction sites. During a leisurely drive on Sunday afternoon, travel around your city and find the homes that are under construction. Be sure that you have a pencil and pad of paper. Make notes of the addresses of the homes under construction that appear to be comparable in style, size, and price range to the home you are planning to construct. You may even want to take a Polaroid® camera along and take pictures of each house as a reminder.

After you have identified the comparable homes in your city, take a day to visit the construction sites and talk with the contractor or the subcontractors who are working on the home. If you find a home where the brick mason is working, stop and talk to the foreman of the crew. Find out the name and telephone number of the company and the company owner and make a note of that information. If you find a house where the drywall sub is working, ask for the same information, and note all this information on the Prospective Subcontractors form.

One note of caution is essential. Before you begin a conversation with the foreman of any crew, check out the quality of the work being performed or which has been performed. Walk around and through the house, checking on the brick seams or the drywall seams, checking on the accuracy of the framing (if visible), checking for signs of quality. You may not wish to use that particular subcontractor, especially if the work is shoddy or of lower quality than you want to have in your house.

If you like what you see, strike up a conversation with the crew chief. Be sure to remember that he will probably know also who the other subs are who are working on this particular job, so do not forget to inquire about other subs whose work you have seen and liked.

In some cases, construction sites will have signs posted at the site informing passersby as to who is performing certain subcontracting functions. Make a note on the Prospective Subcontractors form of those whose work you like and whom you wish to contact.

Use the telephone book. You will recall that, throughout this book, I have emphasized the importance of the Yellow Pages of the telephone book. The phone book is a ready source of information on potential subcontractors, so you should spend some time researching the pages of the phone book for potential subcontractors. Generally, you can find the names and numbers of subcontractors under the headings for the construction specialty. For example, bricklayers will probably be under the heading "Mason Contractors"; drywall installers can be found under the heading "Dry Wall Contractors"; roofers can be found under the heading "Roofing Contractors." You will typically find that the only subcontractor headings that are not found in the phone book include framers, trimout subs and, sometimes, concrete finishers. However, I must note here that the inclusion or non-inclusion of these subcontractors in the Yellow Pages is more often than not a function of the size of the city in which you are located and the amount of competition in the marketplace.

Contact the local home builders' association. Almost every major city in the country has a local home builders' association. The licensed residential contractors in any given area are regular members of such an association. However, these associations also have membership categories for associate members, which might include subcontractors, building supply companies, and other ancillary firms associated with the construction business, such as architects, engineers, and survey companies.

A call to the local home builders' association will result in complete information on any number of subcontractors in your area. You only need to inform the staff at the association that you are constructing a house and wish to use one of their members as a subcontractor. Generally, without hesitation, a list will be provided with the names, numbers, and contact persons. Be aware that a fee may be charged, however small, for this service, since you are not a regular member of the association. Nevertheless, this will give you a ready source of subcontractors for your project.

Visit the Parade of Homes. Much like visiting other construction sites, you should never overlook the vast amount of information available in a Parade of Homes. I recall that my wife and I visited Parades of Homes for four or five years prior to constructing our home. Generally sponsored by the local home builders' association, the Parade of Homes gives you "on the spot" inspection rights and information on all the subcontractors involved in the construction of a particular home. Also, business cards are plentiful, floor plans are abundant, and the licensed contractors are usually on site to explain structural details, if you feel that you need it.

Be sure to carry your Prospective Subcontractors form with you to the Parade site and make notes of the names of those subcontractors whose work you admire. And if their business cards are available, be sure to get them. You can contact these potential subs later.

Visits to Parade sites can help you in determining the interior design of your home as well as traffic patterns and elevation designs. So do not discount the value of visiting Parades of Homes.

Consult with your construction manager. Much more will be written in Chapter 8 regarding the construction manager, but suffice it to say that he is a ready source of information on potential subcontractors. As a licensed contractor himself, he will be able to advise you on the best possible subs and those with whom he can work best.

Investigating the Subcontractors

Now that you have a list of potential subcontrac-

tors for each construction element, you are ready to begin an investigation of the quality of each. Some of this work may have already been done if you have visited other sites and have had an opportunity to visit a Parade of Homes. However, in the absence of these activities, you will want to begin a thorough investigation of the quality, time frame, and pricing structures of each of the potential subcontractors.

Begin this process by making calls to each potential subcontractor. Explain to the person that you wish to look at some samples of his work so that you might select two or three subcontractors with whom you will negotiate. Then ask for the addresses of homes the subcontractor has been associated with or the construction sites of homes with which he is currently involved. Make a note of these addresses in the appropriate box on the Prospective Subcontractors form.

Once this information has been obtained, make visits to all the sites or selected homes or sites with which the subcontractor has been involved. If possible, try to arrange the visits in such a way as to include more than one subcontractor on the same construction site, thereby saving time.

During these visits, make notes regarding the quality of the work in the appropriate section of the Prospective Subcontractors form. These notes will be valuable later. Again, if possible, take along a Polaroid® camera to make instant pictures of examples of the work, making notes on the back of the picture to identify the subcontractor, the address of the home or construction site, and the date the picture was taken. After you have made all the visits you feel are necessary, take the notes and the pictures and select from them no more than three subcontractors whose work you most admired and who you would like to have involved in your construction project. List these in priority order with a 1, 2, or 3 beside each name on the Prospective Subcontractors form. You are now ready to begin the selection process.

Determining Quality Work

Since you will be investigating the quality of the various subcontractors, you may be asking yourself, "What constitutes a quality job, anyway?" This section is intended to help you understand, from the perspective of four subcontractor types, what to look for in terms of quality.

Framer — Check the layout of a house in progress. Look at the way the pre-fabricated portion is actually assembled. If the studs are nailed to the floor sills and plates from underneath, that is a sign of quality. In some cases a good framer will not only nail the wall studs from underneath but will also "toenail" the studs to the sills and plates as well.

Using a tape measure, check the consistency of the space between wall studs. If specifications require that the studs be installed 16 inches on center, the space should consistently be 16 inches.

Check the installation of trusses or any hand construction of roof framing that might be included. Make sure that appropriate and sufficient bracing is included and that the frames do not visibly shake when touched or walked on. Check carefully on the rigidity and sturdiness of the corner braces. Using the specifications of houses in progress, check the measurements of such framing components as windows, doors, and fireplaces. The window frames should measure the exact length and width as required by the plans.

Drywall—This component includes the installation of gypsum board on the walls and ceilings, taping of all seams, sealing all seams with joint compound, sanding and finishing all seams, and finishing coats on the walls and ceilings.

The most telling sign of quality in drywall installation is the lack of need for sanding on the compound applications. Less sanding means less roughness on the paper finish of the drywall board and fewer rough surfaces. The holes cut out for switches, receptacles, and HVAC registers should not be larger than necessary, thus showing a portion of the hole on the outside of a face plate. The stipple finish on the walls should be evenly coated just as is the finish on the ceilings. Joints are "feathered" in such a way as to leave no unsightly bumps or warps. If walls have warps in them, the drywall finish is not good. Make sure all corner beads are smooth, showing no metal, and that the joint compound covering the corner beads is not cracked after drying.

Trimout—Look for doors that are set level in their frames and swing open and shut with ease. A front door that is hard to open and close is a sign of a poorly set door. You should be able to close the front door with one finger.

In looking at doors, inspect carefully around the doors, that is, the space between the door itself and the jamb. If the space around the door is uneven, it is possible that the trim subcontractor did not take the necessary time to set the door properly. A properly and evenly set door will show approximately the same amount of space around the entire door. At least the top of the door will reveal the same amount of space from left to right. Furthermore, door handles and latches will be neatly installed.

Another sure sign of quality in trim work is the joints of wood trim. The trim subcontractor that I used in my home was so good at making joints on the chair rails and floor and ceiling moldings that little or no stained joint compound was required to make the trim appear finished. So check those joints to see how closely they fit with each other.

Bricklayers—Quality in bricklaying is best revealed in three different elements of the bricklaying process. The first is the consistency of space between individual bricks horizontally. As you proceed from left to right, the space between bricks should be even. The space should not be 1 inch between some and 1½ inches between others, or less than one inch between still others. The space between the bricks should be even.

A second element in the quality study for brick-layers is the straightness of the vertical lines. The vertical lines are formed by the joints between bricks laid horizontally. If you stand against a brick wall and look up these joints, they should be as straight as possible. The less straight these lines are, the less attention has been paid to the quality of the work.

A third element in the quality of bricklaying is the use of different styles. Soldiering of bricks makes a neat appearance over windows and doors. Using half-bricks and making creative designs, which are distinctive yet consistent with the style of the house, indicate not only a penchant for creativity but attention to detail and quality.

A fourth indicator I used in my selection process was the amount of wasted mortar and broken bricks lying around the job site during the course of bricklaying. If there are many broken bricks and considerable wasted mortar, this is not a sign of quality, but a sign of inattention. It also costs *you* money, because you will have to purchase additional amounts of sand and bagged mortar mix.

NEGOTIATING WITH SUBCONTRACTORS

The art of negotiating is nowhere better exercised than in dealing with subcontractors. And the point of departure with them is to understand that (1) they are a sub-culture unto themselves and (2) they need the work, sometimes more desperately than they will indicate, to maintain their business.

Most subcontractors, or at least the subcontractors I have dealt with, do not live their lives on a schedule. Their culture dictates that they should arrive at the job site "almost on time," take the necessary breaks from work, and be sure to stop working sufficiently before quitting time to prepare to leave work precisely at quitting time.

They often can make small jobs look like big jobs, requiring considerably more output than is really demanded by the task. They often drink significant amounts of fluid, and converse in a language that either may not be understandable or may be spotted with foul language. If your ears cannot tolerate foul language, don't spend too much time around your subcontractors. If you do, you will be educated to the language of the world.

Many times the subcontractors and their crews exhibit an "I don't care" attitude. While the boss may really be concerned that he and his crew do a good job, often the crew neither possesses nor exhibits that same kind of "good job" attitude. Their only concern, typically, is to "make the day," labor jargon for getting the day finished and going home. If this same "make the day" attitude is characteristic of the owner or boss of the crew, it will be necessary to maintain a fairly close scrutiny of their work, because this kind of attitude tends to be reflected in sloppy or shoddy craftsmanship. If the boss is concerned about quality, the crew will be kept in line generally by the boss, especially if the boss is also the owner of the business.

As you begin your negotiation process, be cognizant of the character of the owner or boss. If you negotiate with the owner and the owner of the business is not also the boss or foreman of the on-the-job crew, then before finalizing any contract with the subcontractor, make it a point to meet the foreman who will be supervising the work on site. This meeting will give you an idea about the degree to which the foreman will see that a quality job is done.

Since you are trying to understand the subcontractor sub-culture, ask direct questions of both the owner and the foreman. Ask questions specific to their trade, questions about their families, what they do in their spare time or recreational time, whether they think they can do this particular job. Get to know as much about each subcontractor as possible in the negotiation process.

I have already mentioned that you should see examples of the work of each subcontractor before beginning negotiations. If it is possible, inquire regarding the location of work in progress and make it a point to visit the site or sites prior to beginning talks with the owner. Such visits, for example, will inform you as to the degree to which a bricklaying crew generates a "mess" on the ground, in corners, or on window sills. Remember that the bigger the mess, the more cleanup is required and more time taken from the schedule of another subcontractor who may come in later. This kind of on-site visit to work in progress is especially helpful with bricklayers, drywall subcontractors, and framers.

Before beginning the negotiation process, it is appropriate to convene with your construction manager to calculate some reasonable ranges in which you feel the subcontractors' estimates should fall. These ranges will be kept with you at all times, but they will not be revealed to any subcontractor.

I can almost hear you asking, "But how are these numbers calculated?" Let me give you some examples. The framer typically will calculate his price based on the total square footage shown in the construction plans. The bricklayers will calculate their price based on a figure, say $32, times the number of thousand bricks to be laid, plus additional charges for brick trim such as you might have around a porch. He will also charge additional for the use of scaffolding if the house is multi-story.

Drywall subs calculate their bids based upon a price per square foot of drywall to be installed. Each sheet of drywall is typically 8 feet by 4 feet or 32 square feet. However, some drywall is produced in 4 X 10 and 4 X 12 sizes. To install one sheet of gypsum board, you simply multiply the price per square foot, say $.20, times the number of square feet, or $6.40 for the installation of the one sheet. As with bricklayers, drywall subcontractors will charge an additional amount for any scaffolding that might be required. The additional scaffolding charges are based upon the number of tiers or sections of scaffolding required.

Roofers calculate bids on the basis of the number of squares (100 square feet) of shingles or roofing materials to be installed. Electricians will calculate their costs generally on the basis of the number of boxes to be installed, with surcharges for specialty wiring.

While these examples indicate the pricing structure for a few of the subcontractors, your construction manager can assist you with others. These are shown only to give you an idea as to the proper means of calculating, within a reasonable range, the cost of several of the construction components.

As you approach negotiation, your attitude should be: *Get the most quality for the least amount of money spent.* If you will maintain that principle, you will be surprised at the results. By this time, through your research, you will have finalized and recorded, in priority order, a list of three subcontractors for each component. Beginning with the first company or individual's name for each component, call the owner and make an appointment to meet with him or her to discuss the project. At this meeting be sure to take along with you a copy of the building plans as approved by the appropriate city, county, or township regulatory agency. Also take a pad and a pencil or pen to record notes to yourself from the meeting.

When you meet, introduce yourself to the owner or person negotiating on behalf of the owner. Explain that you are serving as your own contractor and wish to discuss the job and its cost. Then, using the plans for the house, show him exactly what services you want this subcontractor to perform. If the subcontractor needs a set of plans, be sure to place a set in his hands for calculation of the estimate. Explain any time constraints that might be included in the plan. *Do not mention any cost estimate you might have personally calculated.* Let the subcontractor perform his own calculations and give you a "bid" on the job as he views it. Be aware that many times, the subcontractor cannot provide the bid at this meeting but will need to take the construction documents and calculate his bid. If such is the case, provide a returnable copy of the construction documents to the subcontractor and ask when you might expect to hear from him. Ask for a specific time no later than which you can expect an answer. Make every attempt possible to receive the bid in person and not by mail. It is quite difficult to negotiate a bid by mail, so tell the subcontractor to call you when the bid is ready and you can plan to meet.

Explain also that you wish to have the bid or estimate in writing and signed by the appropriate authorized officer of the business. *Do not accept any bid that is not in writing and signed.* And then *wait.*

If, by the time specified, you have not received an answer, contact the subcontractor by telephone. Make arrangements to meet and receive the bid.

At the meeting where the bid is received, be pleasant with the subcontractor and ask for the bid. He may try to make explanations, but mention that you wish to review the bid first. Study the bid carefully and in conjunction with the estimates you and your construction manager have calculated. Remember, your estimates are rough and are in the form of ranges within which the bid should fall. If the bid is higher than the range you have estimated, begin negotiating by mentioning that the bid is "somewhat higher than had been expected." Explain why this is true and ask if the subcontractor cannot adjust the bid downward by some percentage or dollar figure. You will have budgeted the cost on the Borrower's/Builder's Estimate of Costs form provided by the bank, and you might simply mention that the bid is over the amount allowed by the bank for this component.

Continue this line of questioning and explanation until the subcontractor has agreed to a price you can accept. Then have the subcontractor amend the written bid to whatever extent you have negotiated, and have him sign the docu-

ment and date it. Conclude this meeting by telling the subcontractor that you will be accepting at least two more bids and will be back in touch with him later to make the final determination. You may be surprised to receive a phone call from that subcontractor further lowering the bid. Be open to such calls and register them on the bid sheet.

Make contact with the other two subcontractors whose names have been included in the final three. Proceed with the same process as mentioned above, negotiating the lowest possible bid from each one. And since this is not a sealed bid situation, explain to each one that you may return with a lower bid from a competitor to negotiate further. And even if the subcontractor says, "No, this is my lowest price," take any lower bids to him anyway. Continue going back to each subcontractor with any lower bids until each has maintained that the last numbers are final and no additional negotiations will be conducted. After all bidders have arrived at this conclusion, make your final decision on the subcontractor to be used and place the name, address, telephone number, and contact person on your Project Subcontractors form (see Appendix). Then call the subcontractor and inform him of his selection.

During this conversation, mention that you have developed an approximate timetable for the construction process. Inform him of the estimated date on which you might expect his part of the work to begin. Then keep him informed as to changes in the estimated timetable.

Also mention that you have a construction manager. Inform him of the identity of the construction manager and how he can be contacted. Mention that this person will be in charge of the construction project during those times when you are not around the job site or available. Have the subcontractor direct all questions to you unless you are unavailable. Then direct any questions to the construction manager.

Remember, reputation is also important in any endeavor. Therefore, as a courtesy to the subcontractors not selected, either place a telephone call to each one informing him that he was not selected and why, or write a letter so informing him and expressing appreciation for his cooperation and willingness to participate in your project.

PAYMENTS TO SUBCONTRACTORS

Subcontractors work on a weekly basis. When weather prevents the subcontractor from working, he doesn't work. So it is necessary to space out your payments to the subcontractors over the anticipated period during which the subcontractor is expected to complete his work. Generally, subcontractors will ask for progress payments on Friday of each week. The reason for this regular request is that the funds are needed to pay the subcontractors' work crews their weekly wages. The progress payment should always be paid from a checking account and a careful record of the transaction maintained in your check register and on the appropriate ledger pages. You may wish to use the Ledger forms in the Appendix to maintain this record. The Individual Subcontractor Ledger form is easily understood and begins with the contract price as agreed and includes all progress payments shown as deductions from the contract price. Once the contract price has been paid out, no additional payments are required. Receipts are not essential since you will have a cancelled check for proof of payment. In addition, each payment should be noted in the General Ledger, which begins with the construction loan amount and indicates a progressive balance available at all times. To monitor the progress of construction cost and loan monies available, simply deduct from the General Ledger balance any unpaid bills and/or anticipated expenditures.

Once the subcontractor has completed his work and has been paid in full, you should complete a copy of the Waiver of Lien form and have the subcontractor sign the form. By signing this Waiver of Lien form, the subcontractor is legally signing away any rights to bring civil litigation proceedings against you. That is, he can't sue you! Be sure to keep the contract, ledger sheet, and signed Waiver of Lien together for each subcontractor.

CONCLUSION

I think you're ready now to begin your negotiation with the subcontractors. Remember, *you* will make this an enjoyable experience or a drudgery. I can assure you that it can be one of the most fun experiences you will ever have if you maintain the right attitude. Furthermore, you will likely obtain the finest quality work that is possible from builders in your area for a fraction of the cost to the average home buyer. Good luck and happy negotiating!

8

CONSTRUCTION MANAGEMENT & SCHEDULING
Overseeing the Job

Just the other night I was talking with a man about my experiences as a self-contractor. He said that he wanted to build a house and sure would like to know a way of cutting the cost of its construction. I told him to wait a few months and he would have the benefit of this book to help him to be his own contractor. He said, "No, I don't think I could be my own contractor. To contract my own house would take an inordinate amount of time, and I just don't have the kind of time it would take to accomplish it."

This situation is probably common among most people who must work for a living. Well, do I have a word for that man, *and for you*! The secret to the entire plan, especially for those whose time is severely limited, is contained in this chapter.

While a person might serve as his own contractor and be in charge of the project in terms of authority and permit responsibility, it is best to negotiate with and enlist a licensed contractor to serve as your construction manager. This chapter deals with the job of the construction manager, how to find him, what should be expected of him, what should be included in the contract, the relative costs of such services, and some of the ways in which the construction manager can

be of assistance during the construction phase.

THE CONSTRUCTION MANAGEMENT FUNCTION

Construction management is the process by which the objectives of a construction project are achieved through the coordination of functions by supervisory personnel. In short, construction management is the way to get the job accomplished with the greatest degree of smoothness. The construction manager is there when the self-contractor often cannot be, and he can coordinate the work of several subcontractors at the same time when necessary. The construction manager should be a person who can handle the stress of complicated and often complex circumstances, the irritation caused by subcontractor woes, and the problems created by materials suppliers and inspectors.

OBJECTIVES OF THE CONSTRUCTION MANAGER

While it is impossible to record all the objectives

for which the construction manager might be responsible, the following list will provide a good start.

Quality assurance—The construction manager, because of his background and experience, will be able to provide assurance to the self-contractor that the work is being performed to the highest standards of expectation. He can make suggestions of ways in which certain components might be constructed for added strength or beauty. He can suggest alternatives to materials to add an element of quality to a house. He can utilize his experience as a builder to guard against potential problems before they arise. He can be the eyes and ears of the self-contractor in ways not immediately apparent to the self-contractor.

And it is vital that he serve this function well. To ensure that he is aware of this objective, make it clear to him during the negotiation phase. Be certain that he is cognizant of his responsibility to "look over the shoulder" of the self-contractor to guarantee the highest level of quality from the subcontractors.

On the job—Another objective of the construction manager is to be on the job site or checking on the job during those times when the self-contractor/homeowner cannot be available. If not on the job site, he should be sure that the subcontractors on the job know where he can be found at all times, in case a problem arises.

The on-site work of the construction manager should not substitute for the time of the self-contractor but rather should supplement that time. The self-contractor will establish a pattern of site visits in the early stages of the construction. The construction manager should outline a schedule of visits which can be flexible. This schedule should be shared with the self-contractor so that, if he desires to visit the site at the same time, he may do so. Furthermore, the construction manager should understand that he is on call at all times.

Coordination — The construction manager should be responsible for the coordination of activities on the job site. While the self-contractor may wish to work cooperatively with the construction manager in this function, the manager probably should have the final word on when to call subcontractors, materials suppliers, and inspectors.

This coordination function demands a person with skill to look ahead rather than only at the happenings of the present. Oftentimes, subcontractors require several days of advance notice prior to appearing on a job site. The construction manager will be aware of this and can schedule the subcontractor appropriately, notifying him at the proper time.

Advice—Just as surely as the sun will rise and set tomorrow, you can expect to have changes during the course of construction. Often these changes are not significant, only cosmetic. Nonetheless, they require careful consideration as to viability, safety, and "look."

When cosmetic changes are suggested, the construction manager can advise the self-contractor on the anticipated results of such a change. It is likely that he has seen the results of such a suggestion before and can advise the self-contractor accordingly. When such cosmetic changes do not involve structural members, load factors, or other safety measures, then the construction manager can make suggestions and allow the self-contractor simply to make the final decision regarding the implementation of one of the suggestions.

If the changes involve load factors or structural changes, then the construction manager will certainly earn his money. He can offer advice on the way a particular construction element might be changed. And he may even consult with the designer or an inspector to ensure that any changes suggested would pass inspection by the regulatory agencies.

Let me cite an example that occurred during the

construction of my own house. When the roof trusses were fabricated by the truss company, they were fabricated using incorrect specifications. After returning the roof trusses three times to the truss company for correction, we finally decided to correct the problem on site. After evaluating several alternatives suggested by the construction manager, one alternative was selected to be implemented. The inspector from the city was called to the job site, informed about the present problem, advised of the alternative solution selected, and asked for his opinion as to inspection passage. He informed all of us, the construction manager, the framing subcontractor, and me, that the problem was with the truss company and that we had arrived at a solution that would pass inspection. Needless to say, construction proceeded, using the alternative solution suggested.

Assistance in obtaining subs — You may find yourself in the midst of construction and a subcontractor reneges on his agreement with you. At this point, the construction manager, who has experience in enlisting subcontractors, can suggest competent subcontractors for each specialty. It is then the responsibility of the self-contractor to negotiate with each subcontractor suggested by the construction manager in order to come to an understanding regarding the subcontractor's work, potential schedule, and fee.

CHARACTERISTICS OF THE CONSTRUCTION MANAGER

In seeking a person to fulfill the role of construction manager, it is essential that several factors be taken into consideration. First, the construction manager should be a licensed residential contractor. Only a person who has been in the business knows the problems consistent with construction. Sometimes it is possible to discover a person who was once in the construction business but for one or more reasons no longer actively builds houses. Such a person, if otherwise qualified, would be an excellent candidate for construction manager. If such a person is not available, then search for a licensed residential contractor who is currently in business with whom you may negotiate a construction management contract.

You will definitely want to check on examples of the work of the prospective construction manager. Ask for the addresses of houses the prospective construction manager may have been involved with as the principal contractor. List these addresses in the "Reference Addresses" section of the Construction Manager Locator form in the Appendix. After obtaining these addresses, visit each one and study each house in detail, especially for quality work. If the house is occupied, be sure to explain the reasons for your visit to the occupants and request the opportunity to tour the house.

Second, the construction manager should be a builder whose quality is unquestioned. Your house is very important to you, and you do not want someone working with you who has been known to cut corners on workmanship in order to maintain a schedule or to satisfy a customer's whim. You want a person who builds quality homes, preferably custom homes. (More will be mentioned later about this characteristic.)

The builder whose work quality comes before other considerations is the kind of person you want to employ, if possible. This kind of person will ensure that the work patterns during construction on the home are of the highest quality for the lowest cost. Quality, for him, is of utmost importance, and he will always return to your home with pride in a quality job well done.

The licensed residential contractor you employ as construction manager should be a person of the highest reputation. Now this is not the same as quality building. This characteristic has to do with basic honesty, integrity, and inner character. A builder can have an eye for quality and still be dishonest or unethical in his dealings.

An example of this kind of builder occurred with friends of mine. The builder's reputation for quality was excellent. He was known for constructing high quality homes at prices that were most attractive. And my friends signed a contract to have him build their "dream home." They had purchased a lot in an upscale neighborhood and had worked hard to pay off the lot prior to construction. That way, they could use the equity from the lot to obtain the construction loan.

They signed the contract and construction began. The house appeared to be proceeding as expected, with several construction draws on the loan having been made and provided to the contractor as agreed. When the house was approximately 75% complete, complaints came to the homeowner that a number of the subcontractors' and materials bills remained unpaid. The homeowner knew that the draws had been executed and the money provided to the contractor for the payment of these bills. What the homeowner did not know was that the contractor was using his construction draw funds to pay bills associated with other residential construction which he had in progress.

The end result of this situation was tragic. The contractor declared bankruptcy, making it impossible for the homeowner or the courts to obtain any funds. Furthermore, the Mechanics' Liens on the house became numerous due to the unpaid bills. So not only did the family lose the house they had dreamed of so long, but they also lost the equity in the lot which had been paid in full. They are now residing in an apartment and have begun a new savings program to which they contribute as they can, looking forward to the day when they will have that "dream house."

When considering a person for construction manager, inquire carefully into his reputation as a builder. Check with supply houses he has done business with to ensure that he has a track record of paying his bills. (You need to remember at this point that you will not be delivering draw checks to him. *You* will be paying your

own bills.) Nevertheless, you should have a person with a spotless record in business as your construction manager.

Finally, search for a person who can work cooperatively with others. Some builders work with subcontractors better than others. In fact, there are subcontractors who will tell you that they will not work for Mr. So and So: "He's too unreasonable." But the other side of that coin is that there are contractors from whom many subcontractors will seek work. This is the kind of builder you want to serve as your construction manager.

CONSTRUCTION MANAGER! WHERE ARE YOU?

Before proceeding with the process of finding a construction manager, one factor requires exploration. As is commonly known, there are two types of home builders: speculative and custom. The speculative home builder typically constructs several houses at one time with the idea of selling them to prospects who may or may not exist at the time the house is begun. These builders *speculate* on the possibility of sale.

The second type of builder is the custom builder. He is generally the builder who does not construct a house unless the purchaser is known. He will contract to build the house for a specified price based on the plans and specifications provided by the homeowner. The custom builder deals more directly with a homeowner and so is more personally familiar with the relationship between homeowner and builder. Because of this awareness on the part of the custom home builder, he is more likely to possess the requisite characteristics sought in a construction manager.

Finding a construction manager is probably one of the easiest responsibilities of the self-contractor. As with subcontractors, three major sources come to mind. First, check in the Yellow Pages of the phone book. A review of such headings as

"Home Builders" and "Building Contractors" will disclose the residential builders within the phone listing area. If you are in an area where more than one phone book is used or available, check with each one.

Within these advertisements, note especially those who are listed as custom home builders. These are the contractors you wish to contact. Using the Construction Manager Locator form, write as much of the information on the form as is provided in the phone book. Then call the contractor, asking first if he would consider functioning as construction manager on a residential project. If he responds "yes," then set an appointment to visit and pursue the arrangement further.

Second, call the local home builders' association and ask for a list of contractors who specialize in custom home building. The association will be more than pleased to provide such a list. A modest fee may be charged.

After receiving the list, proceed in the same fashion as with the telephone book prospects. Include the information on the Construction Manager Locator form if the listing is not already on the form from the telephone book search. Call to determine the level of interest in serving as a construction manager and then set an appointment if the answer is favorable. If, in either the phone book search or the association list search, the response to your inquiry is unfavorable, thank the person for his time and proceed to the next prospect. I can assure you that you will find several builders who will be more than happy to serve you as a construction manager.

A final source is friends who may have recently had a custom house constructed. You may wish to inquire from them regarding their satisfaction with the builder and mention that you were thinking about contacting him to serve as a construction manager on your job. Ask the friend for an opinion of such an arrangement. If the response is acceptable, then proceed by adding the name to the Construction Manager Locator

form, if the name is not already on the form. Make contact with the prospect and proceed as instructed earlier.

CONTRACT PROVISIONS

The contract recommended for a construction manager is not a complex one, requiring the time of a lawyer. In fact, a sample Construction Management Contract can be found in the Appendix of this book.

The typical contract, after the "Whereas's" and "Now, Therefore's," contains two parts: (1) the section outlining the responsibilities of the construction manager and (2) the section delineating the responsibilities of the self-contractor/homeowner. These sections are not designed to cover every eventuality but only the major aspects of the scope of work.

Construction Manager's Responsibilities

The general statement governing his responsibilities indicates that the construction manager will administer, manage, and supervise the construction of the house. This general statement is then further explained by the inclusion of several specific responsibilities.

1. Set up the temporary power pole. Every construction site requires the setting of a temporary power pole for electrical service to the power tools used by the subcontractors' labor forces. This power pole can be set in the ground at any time after the site has been prepared; however, power cannot be obtained or connected until the building inspection department has issued a building permit. Taking the building permit number to the power company and filing for temporary power will establish a power source on the temporary pole for which the construction manager is responsible.

2. Supervise and manage all subcontractors obtained by the Owner. Note that the subcontrac-

tors are not obtained by the construction manager. He is only responsible for supervising them and managing their work from the perspective of the self-contractor/homeowner. Only in cases where a subcontractor reneges on an agreement may the construction manager be asked to obtain another sub.

3. Ensure that all subcontractors are on the job at the appropriate and proper time. Usually the construction manager will visit the job site early in the day to ensure that the subcontractors who are scheduled to be on the job are, in fact, on the site, doing their work. If, for any reason, they have not appeared at the scheduled time, it is the responsibility of the construction manager to make contact with the subcontractors and determine why they did not appear. If a problem arises with the subcontractor, then the construction manager will convey that problem to the owner and a resolution will be determined between them.

4. Request and be present at all inspections. While the self-contractor will likely be present also, the construction manager can offer information to the inspector regarding any changes that might have affected the inspection. Furthermore, questions of a technical nature can also be addressed better by the construction manager than by the self-contractor. This situation will put you in a better position with the inspectors than if you were to have the job inspected, technical questions asked, and no ready response.

5. Order materials as required. The materials suppliers will have been selected by the self-contractor and a list of these suppliers provided to the construction manager. His responsibility is to get the materials on the job as they are needed by the subcontractors. If, during the course of construction, he discovers that he has a source of materials that will save the owner money, he should make that information available to the self-contractor so that additional savings can be realized.

6. Other duties may also be added to the responsibilities of the construction manager. The self-contractor should be aware, however, that the construction manager should not be held responsible for duties or items that do not naturally fall within his realm of responsibility. For example, if you need to have doors hung and you do not have a trim subcontractor to perform that function, it is not an inherent part of this contract to ask the construction manager to perform that function at no additional cost. As with any contract, reasonableness is a key factor.

7. If, for any reason, a subcontractor backs out or you discover an element for which you have not obtained a bid, your construction manager may suggest several subcontractors he is familiar with, whom you might contract for the job. He may get you in touch with these people personally so that you can negotiate with them regarding the responsibilities and fees.

Owner's Responsibilities

The second section of the contract relates the responsibilities of the owner. These obligations are generally limited to payment of fees. However, several provisions merit highlighting.

The first element is to provide the construction manager with a list of all subcontractors and materials suppliers with whom you have negotiated. He should be given a copy of the list, which you have compiled, with company names, addresses, telephone numbers, contact persons, and the materials the company will be supplying.

The owner should also accept responsibility for the payment of all subcontractors. The payment of subs and materials suppliers should not be the responsibility of the construction manager. If the self-contractor has not made arrangements with the supplier prior to materials delivery and will not be on the job site at the time materials are delivered, then provide a check in the amount required and allow the construction manager to pay the driver after successful delivery of the materials.

A final provision should be a schedule of payment to the construction manager. The schedule should be identified with the successful completion of specific elements in the construction process. You may wish to arrange the payments in such a way that large amounts are paid at the completion of significant systems inspections such as electrical or plumbing, with final payment made only upon the successful final inspection and awarding of a certificate of occupancy.

CONSTRUCTION MANAGEMENT FEES

The construction manager should be employed or enlisted much like the designer. On whatever basis the fee is established, it should be fixed rather than variable. Sometimes the construction manager will desire a fee based upon a percentage of the cost of the house. Since your house is being self-contracted, this may be difficult to determine unless you base the fee on the construction loan amount. Furthermore, as with the designer, no fee should be directly related to the cost of the house.

You will probably be surprised at the fee you can negotiate with a construction manager. No construction manager "worth his salt" merits more than 10% of the estimated costs or construction loan amount. That is the absolute ceiling to consider. *Remember that these comparisons to the cost of the house are for calculation purposes only.* Often it is better to establish that fee at no more than 5% of the estimated costs or the construction loan amount. In my case, I was able to negotiate a construction management contract with one of the highest quality custom home builders in my area for a fee that amounted to only 3.8% of the construction loan amount. My best advice is to negotiate the very best price with the very best prospect. And write that fee into the contract with a specifically outlined schedule of payment.

CONCLUSION

As mentioned at the beginning of this chapter, choosing a construction manager is important because it is the secret of the entire plan. *And it works!* It is not necessary to convince the building inspection department that you can build your own house; often state legislation makes provision for that situation. But you will be required to convince a mortgage company that they can comfortably invest their construction funds with you with the assurance that you can bring the job to a successful conclusion. The most convincing argument with the mortgage company is to provide them with the name of and contract with a licensed residential (custom) builder. You will find the mortgage company much more likely to approve your request under these circumstances.

Regardless of the value of the construction manager toward obtaining construction loan funds, he can also serve a very practical purpose, namely, assisting the self-contractor with technical questions the self-contractor probably would not be in a position to address knowledgeably. By employing a construction manager, complex structural problems can be resolved with a minimum of difficulty; whereas, without such management, unnecessary delays might be encountered and valuable time may be lost.

9

AMENITIES
Controlling the Cost

If you were to ask me what I want to include in my home, I might say something like Italian marble floors, gold leaf chandeliers, mahogany trim, finished wood flooring, Florentine marble bathroom fixtures, or stone statues on the lawn. More realistically, I would probably say a sauna, tennis courts, swimming pool, hot tub, wainscoting, wallpaper, stained trim, and the like. Wow! What a list!

But the cost of a home is probably most controlled by the amenities that are included. Marble, parquet, cabinetry, carpeting, porcelain, artwork, statuary, wood finishes, swimming pools, saunas, tennis courts, lawn and fire prevention sprinkler systems — all such amenities typically control the cost of the home. If these costs can be controlled, then the overall cost of the home can be controlled. This chapter discusses amenities, the relative additional cost of selected amenities, how to control the cost of some of these amenities, and the contribution they make to both the expense and the "look" of the home.

To get a grasp of the suggestions in this chapter, it is essential that you understand the terminology used. Throughout this chapter, the term "amenity" or "amenities" will be employed. And it is important to note the difference between "amenities" and simply "quality."

DEFINING THE TERMS

When reference is made to amenities, the reference is typically to an item which, by its very nature, adds significant cost and character to a house. It is best described as an "extra." That is, it is not an essential or vital part of the construction, but rather it is a highly desirable addition.

Amenities are not just "high quality" items. Some form of quality exists in all components of the construction project. Some of these components may be of high quality construction and design while others may be of lower quality construction and design. But quality of product and amenities are not synonymous.

In reviewing a construction job, two types of amenities come into focus. This section will address both types of amenities as well as their relative cost and the contribution they make to the home.

AMENITIES RELATED TO NECESSITIES

Obviously, all homes include certain necessary elements or components. These might be floors, ceilings, bathrooms, glass, doors, hardware, and other such necessities without which the house could not be built. However, there are also associated with many of these necessities items that might best be described as amenities.

Floors

Every home needs floors. Some people live in houses with bare concrete floors, but most people want to have the floors constructed of wood and finished or covered with an attractive floor covering. Some of these floor coverings would be defined as amenities. For example, you may wish to cover your floors with expensive carpeting. This does not constitute an amenity; it is simply your desire to have a high *quality* covering on the floor. On the other hand, if you wish to have marble on your floor, then that would be considered an amenity. Why? Primarily because of the cost of materials and the added cost of installation. The most expensive carpet materials can cost as much as $50 per square yard, with vinyl coverings typically somewhat less expensive. However, marble, at its least expensive, is approximately $10 per square foot (purchased from the manufacturer), making a square yard valued at $90. And whereas the cost of installation of carpet and vinyl is included in the price of the materials, the cost for installing marble is extra.

Parquet and oak wood floors also would be considered amenities that would add significant extra cost and character to a house. The added cost would be reflected in higher prices paid for the materials and the extra labor cost for installation.

Ceilings

Actually, the parts of the ceiling considered to be amenities are the design and the finish. Notable added cost can be expected from such designs as recessed ceilings, vaulted ceilings, odd-shaped ceilings, or bevels. Furthermore, immense added cost can be expected if hand-finished ceilings are included. Recessed ceilings, vaulted ceilings, odd-shaped ceilings, and beveled ceilings generally require additional framing, thereby adding materials and labor cost. Hand-finished ceilings, which were popular in the forties and fifties, can still be found designed into some homes. These ceilings require special plaster board as well as the expert craftsmanship of a plasterer who has the ability to put designs into the ceiling. The added cost of hand-craftsmanship is difficult to measure and should be investigated before employing a subcontractor (if you can find one) to put such a finish on the ceilings.

Trim Finishes

Because of the cost factor, licensed contractors will typically install paint-finished trims in a house. Paint finish simply means that the cabinetry, as well as the moldings around the floors, ceilings, doors, etc., is finished with opaque paint rather than stain and varnish. The reason for such installations is that the cost of paint-finished materials is less than that of stain-finished materials. When the manufacturer constructs a door frame or molding, for example, he can splice separate pieces together to manufacture longer footage. The seams of such materials are easily seen, so the materials are much less expensive and used in homes only where an opaque paint will be employed to cover the seams.

In the case of stained trim, materials are extruded in a more continuous flow so that fewer seams are manufactured into the materials. If the materials were formed with many seams, the seams would be revealed through the clear finish. Therefore, stain-finished trim materials are more expensive to purchase and cost significant added dollars to finish and install. Nevertheless, the added character of stained trim, as well as the lower cost of maintenance, makes stained trim well worth considering.

Windows

When contemplating windows for your home, you may wish to investigate the relative cost difference between single-paned windows and insulated or thermal break windows. While the cost of thermal break windows is generally higher, the savings in utilities often can offset such expense within a relatively short period of time.

But thermal break windows are so common today that they really are not considered an amenity. However, such items as stained glass or specialty glass would be considered amenities. Stained glass, so popular in the early part of the century, can add charm and personality to any home. But the self-contractor/homeowner must consider carefully the added cost of such windows before embarking on commissioning windows to be constructed. While the cost of the stained glass windows varies with the region of the country and the artisan, typically the least cost involved in the fabrication of stained glass windows is $100 per square foot. This means that if you want to have a stained glass window in your bathroom, for example, measuring 48 inches square, you can expect to pay a minimum of $1,600 for that window. And that amount excludes the price of lamination. Lamination is recommended for all stained glass windows, for in this process the stained glass is sandwiched between two pieces of tempered glass and placed in a metal window frame for installation. Window fabrication companies that manufacture windows for residential use can perform such fabrications. If you are skilled in stained glass, you might want to include it in your home. You can design and construct the artistic portion of the window yourself, and then the cost for lamination added to your cost is not much greater than the cost of a purchased thermal break window.

Other Necessities

When selecting items with which to build your house, be careful to consider the added cost of amenities related to such items as bathroom and kitchen fixtures. While gold looks expensive and exclusive, the cost of gold faucets can be prohibitive, especially in light of the fact that brass will often achieve the same effect at great savings. Even greater savings can be expected from the use of chrome fixtures. In addition, the use of Jacuzzi-type tubs can cost as much as three times the price of a 60-inch standard tub.

Marble basins and bathroom counter tops are another area where amenities can add cost to a house. The added value of these items is not likely to measure up to the cost they will add to the house. When determining cost, consider such substitutions as Corian®, which provides the same marble appearance but at great savings.

Finishes in a home offer the self-contractor the greatest challenge for savings. From the type of tile used to line the bathroom walls to the use of mirrored doors—all these items can be considered amenities that will add both cost and value to the house.

AMENITIES AS UNNECESSARY EXTRAS

To this point, the discussion has focused upon items associated with the necessary elements or components in a house. Conversely, there are amenities that would be considered unnecessary and that add immense cost to a house. While no lengthy discussion is required on these items, they do bear mentioning.

Swimming Pool

Ask almost any appraiser of real estate, and that person will tell you that the added value of a swimming pool is almost always less than the cost of installing it. The value is generally less. Furthermore, the self-contractor must reflect upon various types of swimming pools available, each one at greater cost. Consider the vinyl pool, a gunite pool, or a fully-formed concrete pool. In each case, there are increasing costs associated with it, the least starting at approximately $6,000, depending upon the part of the country in which you live.

Tennis Courts

Tennis courts are wonderful sources of exercise, but can you afford to have one constructed? The minimum cost is approximately $10,000, depending upon the section of the country in which you live. They require several subcontractors to complete the job and will add to your responsibility as the self-contractor. As with swimming pools, the value added is seldom equal to their cost.

Ceiling Fans

Careful reflection is required when considering the installation of ceiling fans. The added cost is generally from the electrical subcontractor as well as the potential extra expense of the fans against the use of standard lighting fixtures. Nevertheless, ceiling fans *can* be a valuable investment in the long run. This is due primarily to the savings in utility bills they can potentially generate. Furthermore, careful shopping can often result in excellent savings, sometimes bringing the cost of good quality ceiling fans and light kits to a level almost equal to the use of lighting fixtures alone.

Miscellaneous Extras

The list of unnecessary amenities in a house is almost as endless as your imagination. And while the list here is not all-inclusive, it does serve to provide examples of the kinds of extras that might be considered for a house. Such items as a hot tub, a sauna, a weight room, an outside gazebo, entrance gates, and outside lighting—all of these items will add dollars to the cost of your house. If you can afford these items, then contemplate including them. However, use your skills and knowledge from this book to reduce the cost of such items to their lowest level.

HOW TO REDUCE THE COST

In the early stages of house planning, it is reasonable to establish a wish list of all the items you may want to include in your new home. Nothing should be discarded. Leave that action until later in the process when cost estimates have been calculated. List the desirable items in priority order, then, as you plan your home, obtain estimates of the cost of these items. Keep this information handy as you plan.

Since most of the items related to necessities are finishing items, you can wait until the final design has been decided to begin making decisions relative to the amenities. Once the design is determined, begin the cost estimate using the Borrower's/Builder's Estimate of Cost form. Once the raw costs have been estimated, you are in a position to begin calculating finishes and amenities associated with these necessities. If, after these estimates are added, funds remain available from your overall cost estimate, then you may consider adding the amenities from the unnecessary extras list.

There are several ways to reduce the cost of amenities. You may wish to pursue each one for each separate amenity or you may choose to focus on one or two approaches. The important factor will be to satisfy yourself that you can reduce the price no lower than the last price obtained. When that situation occurs, then you can decide whether you wish to include the amenity in your house.

The following actions or combinations of actions provide a beginning point for helping reduce the cost of amenities in your house. While you may think of additional ways to reduce such costs, those listed have been proven by experience.

Check with manufacturers. By doing some research in the local library, you can find manufacturers of materials and make direct contact with them. Requirements by manufacturers differ as to the conditions under which you may make purchases directly, so you will want to get explicit information on the process of making such purchases. Once you know the requirements of the manufacturer, you can begin to plan how to achieve your purpose with those requirements in mind.

In my experience, I not only purchased the doors, frames, and trim materials from a local wholesaler for only 10% more than the wholesale price but, through this wholesaler, I was also able to purchase marble flooring which was installed in the foyer of my house. The cost savings on the doors, frames, and trim materials were adequate to allow me to include marble, which was purchased directly from the manufacturer in another state. The pink, white, and gray marble now covers the floor of our foyer, an exquisite amenity to our home.

Shop around. In cases where you can make purchases locally, be sure to shop among the various suppliers or companies and compare cost. Much as you might comparison shop for groceries, you can comparison shop for materials, supplies, and those extras that you might want to include. As you shop, be certain that you provide identical information to each subcontractor or supplier. You should not get in the position of comparing "apples to oranges," by using one set of specifications for one and a separate set for another. Keep a list of the costs provided by each subcontractor or supplier on the Amenities Pricing form in the Appendix. As you near the time when the final estimate of cost is to be determined, you can use the information to decide whether the amenity will be included in the construction project.

Check with retailers who specialize in used materials. For example, if you wish to have a beautiful wooden mantel and wooden side pilasters for your fireplace, you might consider shopping in the used furniture or antique stores. Sometimes these items can be purchased on the used market for prices far less than the cost of having a subcontractor build them. By taking a Saturday to browse through the used furniture and antique stores, you can uncover bargains that will add character to your home at costs that will astound your friends. Furthermore, you will add some fun and spice to your life.

Negotiate. My feeling is: Never take the first figure as absolute. There is always room for negotiation. Negotiation includes a willingness to ask the person for a lower price. If you are afraid to request a lower price, you will not be a good negotiator. However, if you realize the potential savings that may be realized, then lift your head high and ask the salesperson, "How about 10% more off the price?" If he refuses, then make a note of the final price on your Amenities Pricing form. Then tell the salesperson that you will be shopping around for a better deal, but you may also be back later if this is the best price. Then actually shop for a better deal. When you find one, return to each business, inform each of the results of your survey, and ask whether they would like to match or better the prices you have obtained. If they match the prices, then you must decide if the quality, reputation of the company, and warranty assurances are also equal. If not, walk away. If so, then make a note and check with the next dealer. Continue this process until all dealers have stated their final prices. Then, after considering quality, dealer reputation, and warranty assurances as well as price, make your final decision both as to the inclusion of the amenity in your construction project and the dealer from whom you potentially will make the purchase.

CONCLUSION

Amenities in a home can provide extra character, quality, and warmth. And the inclusion of amenities need not be forfeited simply because the self-contractor thinks that they will cost too much. Investigate the possibilities before making a decision. You may be favorably surprised. By using a common sense approach, you can turn your new house into a veritable palace for considerably less than you might expect.

10

PITFALLS OF SELF-CONTRACTING
Enduring the Process

"My wife and I almost got a divorce over this house." "I don't think I will ever get involved in building another house as long as I live." "I think it's just better to find something you can live with that someone else has already built and buy it." Sound familiar? I can't tell you how many times I have had friends make one of these kinds of statements to me.

Or how about this one from a well-known, licensed residential contractor when he was told that I was planning to self-contract my house. "You'll be sorry. If you've never built a house before, you will get yourself into a mess out of which you can't be redeemed. You're getting into a situation that will be nothing but an embarrassment for you. I would suggest you get a licensed contractor to build that house rather than trying to do it yourself. You just don't have the skills to do it."

Now, to say that a home can be self-contracted without frustration, difficulty, problems, or headaches would be a gross misstatement of fact. Every self-contractor can expect the same kinds of problems that befall a licensed contractor who is in the business to make money. This chapter describes some of the pitfalls and woes

that beset the self-contractor and how to deal with them. The chapter also provides some mental health counseling to help the future homeowner maintain the proper attitude for functioning as a self-contractor.

EXCHANGING BLAME

Whenever there is more than one person involved in any kind of project, you can expect problems to arise. And such is the case with constructing a house. With subcontractors, material suppliers, laborers,
possible to organize in such a way as to ensure that each responsible party will do his job efficiently, effectively, and on time.

Sometimes there is a job to be performed when no subcontractor is willing to accept the responsibility to perform it. For example, a dishwasher needs to be installed. Is the installation the responsibility of the electrician who must connect it to the power source, the plumber who must attach the water and waste lines, or the company providing or selling the dishwasher? You can almost bet that not any one of the three will claim responsibility for its installation.

Another example of the lack of responsibility might be the installation of lighting fixtures. Once the fixture is installed and power is connected, if the light fixture does not operate properly, who should be called to correct the problem? The electrician who installed the fixture, the wiring, and the switch or the company who sold the fixture to the homeowner? The electrician is going to say that the problem is with the fixture and that it should be replaced by the company selling it to the contractor. The selling company will say that it is the responsibility of the electrician who wired the house and installed the fixture and its ancillary or connecting parts.

It is a fact of life that throughout the construction process, as problems arise in which two or more subcontractors may have been involved, no subcontractor will accept the blame or responsibility for correcting such problems. Inevitably, each will blame the other and attempt to cast that responsibility off to another subcontractor.

As a self-contractor, it is your responsibility to analyze the problem with your construction manager and seek to resolve the issue with the subs. In any case, you should be able to analyze the problem and arrive at a reasonable decision regarding responsibility. Then have your construction manager go to the subcontractor whose responsibility you have determined it is to correct the problem. Do not threaten legal action or any other type of action unless the subcontractor completely refuses to accept the responsibility for the problem.

TO SHOW OR NOT TO SHOW

Probably one of the more common problems for all contractors, whether self-contractors or licensed contractors, is having subcontractors and their crews not show up for work when prom-

ised. As you schedule work for each subcontractor, it is important that the subcontractor and his crew appear at the job site ready for work at the time specified. I can tell you, as a matter of fact, that such will not always be the case.

Let me cite you one example from the construction of my house. As I have suggested in this book, I obtained subcontractors and contracted with them before construction was ever initiated. That means that I had already obtained and scheduled the services of a drywall contractor prior to beginning construction. On the day in the construction process when the drywall contractor was to begin work, no one appeared. Neither the contractor nor any member of his crew showed for work even though scaffolding and other materials had been delivered to the job site.

After several days of no appearance at the job site, I called the drywall contractor and advised him that his services were no longer required. Great situation, wasn't it? At that point I contracted with a "friend" who had experience in the installation of drywall and had some spare time to work on my house. After three days of installation time, he realized he was literally in over his head and bailed out on me, leaving me in less than midstream.

I then called yet another contractor who agreed to be at the job site the next day. On the following day, the drywall contractor did not appear. Nor did he appear the second day. During the second day, I obtained the services of a fourth drywall contractor who did appear. I then called the third contractor and told him to forget coming to my house, if he had ever planned to come. The fourth and last contractor performed the task at a price competitive with the other estimates and furthermore, the job was extremely well done. I was grateful for a competent job. However, I could have done without all the hassle of "no-shows" and incomplete work.

It is important to note that the situation in which

subcontractors do not show for work is certainly not uncommon. When you sign the contract with the sub, you may wish to make absolutely certain that the contractor will be able to meet the proposed schedule you have established for the project. Or he should at least be able to meet that schedule within a two- or three-day period, assuming there are no weather delays or unforeseen emergencies.

HOW CAN I WORK WITH NO MATERIALS?

Another pitfall, which typically is the responsibility of someone other than the self-contractor, is the materials supplier. You may find yourself in need of certain materials your supplier does not currently have in inventory. This, too, can cause a delay, especially if the materials cannot be ordered from another supplier.

AHA! IT'S RAINING!

Weather will always be a factor in the construction time of a house. But the weather also plays a part in the time subcontractors stay on the job. If a subcontractor appears at the job site in the morning and finds that the weather is rainy, he generally will take his crew and depart for another job site or for home. If the rain stops ten minutes after he leaves with the crew, that's too bad. The day is lost. Generally, subcontractors will not wait around for a change in the weather.

One of the more common delays in any construction project is bad weather. And you can usually expect inclement weather sometime during the course of construction. No one has control over the weather, and until a house is "dried in," that is, it has a weatherproof roof over the structure, bad weather is a factor. Once a house has been dried in, weather becomes less of a factor except in those cases where humidity

becomes a detriment. Nevertheless, expect weather to become a delaying factor during the time of construction.

THAT DARNED INSPECTOR!

Two pitfalls that relate to the building inspector occur when a project is underway. The first of these is the scheduling of the inspector. Most inspectors arrive quite early at their offices and are thus able to begin inspections early. So if they are not contacted early in the morning, it is usually the afternoon before they can be re-contacted for inspections. And there are times when inspections are scheduled and are not performed at the scheduled time. In fact, most inspectors I have dealt with will only provide a range of times during which they expect to arrive at the job site. If they do not make the morning "round," then they try to arrive at your job site in the afternoon. If they are unable to perform an inspection during a particular day, then everything must stop until that inspection is conducted, resulting in more lost production time.

The second pitfall relating to inspections deals with their results. At times, inspectors have "pet peeves" and may become picky about certain items on their personal inspection checklist. They may wish to have construction done a specific way and hope to see that specific kind of construction when they arrive to conduct the inspection. When items being inspected are not exactly the way an inspector desires, he may demand that modifications be made to the item in question. These modifications require additional work time and reduce the productive time in which work might otherwise be accomplished.

HOW MUCH LONGER, PLEASE?

All of these pitfalls contribute to yet another inevitable problem—the length of the construction time. While you may have estimated the period of construction with absolute precision, and while you may have tried to maintain a perfect schedule, you will always find that the construction time for the project will be longer than expected, if only by a few days. One of the reasons for such miscalculation is the pitfalls that are being discussed in this chapter. There is no way to predict the weather, the action of subcontractors, or the delays of materials. So the best way to deal with this pitfall is to understand from the beginning that the construction project will require more time than you expect. If the final construction period is shorter than expected, you should be happy with the results. If the project takes longer than anticipated, you can be happy because the project time frame was about as you really expected—that is, longer than you thought would be necessary.

THE UNEXPECTED

You have probably heard someone say with regard to building a house, "Expect the unexpected." Well, the advice is true. Also, Murphy's Law seems to be etched in stone when it comes to house construction, because if something can go wrong, it usually can and will.

Expect unexpected expenditures. You can be as sure as the sun rises and sets that there will be expenditures you did not think of or expect. For example, during the estimating phase of my home, I failed to take into account the fact that city or county building codes called for the disposal of building waste into an open dumpster. Such an expenditure can amount to several hundred dollars over the period of construction. Furthermore, an on-site portable toilet was not figured into the overall cost of the house. And these facilities, too, can cost considerable funds when they must be on site for three to six months or more.

Expect the house to appear smaller than it really is. When a house is laid out on the ground with batter boards in place, the footings are dug and poured, the slab or floor portion of the

house has been installed, you can be sure that your spouse or someone else will tell you how much smaller the house is going to be than expected. When the slab had been poured on our new house, I remember that my wife complained about the kitchen being so much smaller than she desired and that the master bedroom was really hardly worth using as a master bedroom because it was so small. During the period of construction room sizes can be deceptive. A floor plan on paper is considerably greater than it appears in the early stages of construction. In fact, you really will not get a proper perspective on the size until after the drywall has been installed. So don't be deceived by what appears to be a smaller size than planned.

Expect everyone to offer advice. From your family to your friends, everyone will have advice to offer. You can expect to receive advice on everything from floor plan changes to elevation alterations and decoration alternatives. Some of the advice will be worthy of consideration, some of the advice will be worth little or nothing. My advice is to listen attentively, smile, and then do what you think is best for your situation.

Beware of "friends" who want to help. Friends who start out with you in constructing your home may not be friends in the end. Either they are unintentionally unhelpful or their "cost savings" recommendations end up costing you more money. Friends probably should not be enlisted to assist with any of the construction. Just wait until you have a finished product and let them come to an open house.

Expect someone not to follow your house plan specifications. When this occurs, delays may result while the job is redone. Or even worse, design changes, which also take time, may result in order to compensate for major mistakes. This very problem occurred with our house when a subcontractor wrongly constructed a portion of the roof truss system, the outcome of which was time-consuming and costly delays, not only involving the framer, who was confused and frustrated, but also the architect and HVAC subcontractor. Remember, there is always someone who did not pay attention when his teacher taught him to follow instructions.

SOME MENTAL HEALTH TIPS

The construction of a house can be a positive or negative experience, depending upon the attitude with which the self-contractor enters the project. As long as the self-contractor is aware that there will be problems—not insurmountable problems, but problems nonetheless—he can successfully construct his own house for considerably less money than through a licensed contractor. However, developing and maintaining a proper attitude is the major step in realizing the dream. For if you successfully construct the house but have a nervous or mental breakdown or a fracture in the family structure, then the effort was certainly not worth the savings.

In this section, I want to offer some mental health tips for the successful self-contractor. These tips are not written in priority order; rather, together they comprise an appropriate and acceptable approach to enduring self-contracting. It is my hope that the experience of self-contracting could be so enjoyable and rewarding that you might want to repeat the experience at some time in the future.

Take time to prepare for the experience. The beginning point in preparation is reading this book and becoming aware of the positive and negative possibilities related to the project. If you are aware of some of the types of problems you might encounter, you are more likely to be able to deal with them successfully and with a minimum of stress.

Investigate every aspect of the experience before embarking on the project. And if you find that you cannot cope with negotiating on materials or negotiating contracts with subcontractors or analyzing problems, you might want to abandon

your project and let a licensed contractor do the job for you. However, if you are good at working with people and can spend some time each day reviewing the progress of the work, if you enjoy negotiations and are not afraid to ask for discounts, if you like to work with details and can analyze problem situations, then you possess the psychological makeup required to bring a home construction project to successful completion.

Have patience. You have probably heard the adage, "Haste makes waste." Well, that adage certainly applies to the construction of a house. You must maintain an attitude of patience to avoid creating problems and stress. Furthermore, if you are patient, you are not easily disturbed and do not easily become overwrought by the small problems that arise frequently during construction.

Not only will you need patience simply doing the project, but you will also need patience with the subcontractors. When a sub does not show up for work, or when a sub shows up for work, works fifteen minutes and leaves, or when the brick masons are on the job and the bricks have not been delivered, you muster all your patience to deal with these stressful times. So you will need patience not only to deal with the project itself but also to deal with the subcontractors, their crews, and others who have responsibility in the project.

You will need patience to deal with your family. Your family will probably mention often how slowly the work seems to be going and the fact that the house won't be ready on time for a scheduled occupancy. Remember that their impatience is due to a lack of knowledge of what is actually being done and how much additional work is yet to be done. Your patient attitude will go a long way toward soothing their minds, calming their nerves, and offering reassurance.

Patience will be a special virtue when dealing with inspectors. While you may totally disagree with a demand by an inspector, you will encounter fewer problems if you keep a cool head and a patient mind. For whether you agree or disagree, especially if it is a matter of law, once the inspector has determined a requirement that he feels is not being met, it is best to capitulate and complete the task rather than argue and make a nuisance of yourself. I can assure you that, in a case where you lose your patience with the inspector on a matter of law, you will lose much more in delays, additional demands, and "picky" inspections.

Be aware of the "hurry up and wait" principle. In the construction of our home, it seems we often were told by the subcontractors to obtain parts, supplies, or appliances because they were needed immediately. We would take time out and juggle schedules in order to make selections and purchase items for immediate delivery. Then we would discover that the subcontractor was not in such a hurry for the materials after all, or he didn't even show up on time for installation. It just seemed that we hurried up just to get to wait again.

Don't sell a house on condition of occupying the new house on schedule. Many people, in fact most people, must sell one house to have the funds to put into another house. However, it is never wise to sell a house with the expectation that you will be able to occupy the new house at the time you must vacate the sold house. The reason is that too many times the unexpected occurs, the time schedule is interrupted, and occupancy of the new house is delayed. When this situation arises, stress is increased in the family.

It is much better to enter into a construction project with the idea that a few days or even weeks may be spent in neither house. Contingency plans should be made during the preconstruction period for just such an eventuality. If you are prepared before it happens, then when you must vacate the sold house and live for a short time in an apartment, motel room, or rental house, you are not overly stressed at the prospect.

Unless you over-compensate when preparing the project schedule, it is highly unlikely that you will complete the house at the time that you anticipate. For many of the reasons stated earlier in this chapter, delays develop, and if weather becomes a factor, sometimes lengthy delays can result. The stress of the situation is reduced, therefore, if you have made contingency living arrangements in case the house is not complete at the time you may be required to vacate the sold house.

Be persistent. In dealing with subcontractors and materials suppliers, you must be persistent. Each one will make every effort to thwart your abilities to "get the price down." But be persistent, especially in areas where home building has slowed somewhat. You are in a "win-win" situation.

Be persistent also when paying subcontractors and suppliers. When the time arrives to make final payment, insist that the appropriate, authorized representative of the subcontractor or materials supplier sign the Waiver of Lien form (see Appendix). Before you present a check to the person, insist on a signature on the Waiver of Lien. If he is not the appropriate signatory, give him the form and have him get the owner or authorized representative to sign it. When the signature is obtained, *then* present the check. It is your right to have the Waiver of Lien signed before handing over any final funds. This Waiver of Lien will avoid any possibility of the subcontractor or materials supplier placing a Mechanic's Lien on your new house.

Be firm but flexible. Maybe a better way to describe this tip is to be *sensible in your dealings*. There will come a time when you must be firm in your stance on an issue. When the time for firmness comes, do not hesitate to remain firm in your position. However, if there is room for compromise, be sensible enough to recognize the situation and flexible enough to give up a part of your position to whatever extent is possible without compromising your convictions.

An excellent example of this tip came for me in the purchase of drywall materials from a supplier. After delivery and even partial installation, I went to pay the supplier for the drywall materials. At this point the desk attendant for the drywall supplier attempted to charge me more than I had been quoted. I simply noted that I was not going to pay more than I had been quoted. There was little they could do. I offered them a check in exchange for their authorized signature on the Waiver of Lien form. Needless to say, they provided the signature, and I provided a signed check forthwith.

Another example will illustrate the flexible part of this tip. When dealing with drywall subcontractors, I encountered supreme difficulty. I attempted to negotiate with the final subcontractor for a price of $.17 per square foot for installation. He told me that his price was $.19 per square foot. I had negotiated a real good deal of $.17 per square foot with the first subcontractor I had dealt with. But lots of good that negotiation did! He never showed up for work, and I finally fired him. This final subcontractor remained firm in his price. Because the difference in price was less than $100 total, I weighed the potential delay with the additional cost and discovered that the additional cost was little price to pay to avoid undue delays. I was sensible enough to be flexible in my approach to a tough problem.

CONCLUSION

You will make this experience exactly what *you* want it to be. It can become for you the most frustrating, debilitating, and time-consuming experience of your life. Or you can allow it to be an enjoyable experience that will lead you to say later, "You know, I'd like to build another house. That was fun!"

As you begin to consider building your own house, take into account the problems you might encounter. Ponder carefully your willingness to put in the necessary time to accomplish the task over the months and weeks required. Weigh with concern the value-added quality of your new home over the time you will invest. But also judge the value of personal accomplishment once the project is complete. *You will never be the same!* Just remember: Don't let the pitfalls become excuses for giving up; turn them into resolve to keep on going!

11

MOVING DAY
And They Lived Happily Ever After

Moving day! What a time to rejoice! All of the woes and problems encountered during construction suddenly fade into obscurity on the day you move into the home that you have so methodically and meticulously planned and constructed. The joy of that day is described in this chapter along with what might be expected during the first year in your new home. This chapter also deals with the problems that might be encountered after moving day and specific actions to take to deal with such problems.

MOVING DAY

The day has come to move. For the first time in your life you will have enough closet space to hang all those clothes you just don't have the heart to give away. Finally you will have enough storage space to store all those "pack rat" boxes and "white elephant" gifts you have accumulated over the years. There's even furniture that you really don't want anymore but are not willing to give up. So now you have the space to store it without having to rent a mini-warehouse.

The movers come, pack your belongings, and hurry off to that new residence you show off with pride. From cloud nine you tell the movers that you built the house. "Isn't it great?" you say. All the while the movers are continuing their work, moving in the furniture and the endless supply of boxes containing the accumulation of years of family history.

Finally, everything is inside the house. At least that much is done. Now the real work begins—putting every item in its rightful place. After two days, the house already feels familiar and homey. All the furniture is placed, and there is no clutter on the floors or in the closets. Your dream has come true at last!

But wait. The light bulb in the living room doesn't work. And this is only the beginning. Much more can and will happen in a house that is not yet "test driven." And just as sure as the sun will rise tomorrow, something—some unexpected event, some unforeseen problem, or some unanticipated headache—will occur. You might as well sit and wait for it to happen.

It is not possible to list all the problems that could befall the newly experienced self-contractor. I will mention only a few in this chapter, and these are the ones that I experienced in the first year of my occupancy. I think you will find them to be representative of the kinds of difficulties you will likely encounter during that first year.

MAJOR PROBLEMS

Leaks

When the first rainstorm blows through your area, be sure to take that opportunity to inspect your house for leaks, especially the ceilings under the roof. That is, if your house is two-story, be sure to inspect the ceilings of the second floor. If possible, it is best to enter the attic and inspect it visually for possible leaks. Sometimes leaks occur but are not severe enough to seep through the ceiling. So inspect the underside of the roof decking for possible small leaks during that first rainstorm.

If you discover a leak, note its location, using chalk or some type of marker, and place a mark around the portion of the decking or ceiling where the leak occurs, and call the roofer. If a leak does happen, it will usually be around a break in the roof where metal flashing has been installed to prevent such leaks. These breaks are usually around vents and chimneys. Be sure to search there first.

You need to be aware, however, that leaks not only occur in the roof but in other places as well. During the first rainstorm after we occupied our house, I found water pouring through the screw holes to the blind clamps on two bedroom windows, one on the second floor and one on the lower floor. I immediately investigated the problem in the attic. The best assessment that could be made—which has since been confirmed—was that the attic vent fan on the south end of the house pulled a driving southbound rain into a wall attic vent, causing the water to puddle until it overflowed and poured down the wall sec-

tion where the two windows were located. Such problems are rather complicated and require careful evaluation as to cause and resolution.

Plumbing Problems

If properly installed, you will likely have less problems with the plumbing in your house than with any other major system. Nevertheless, during the winter season, the plumbing will be severely tested, especially if you live in an area where the temperatures go below freezing. Frozen pipes are not a part of the unwritten warranty (see the section later in this chapter on the unwritten warranty) that accompanies the work of subcontractors on your house. This act of nature will require you to have your designer carefully design the specifications for the house to avoid as many such problems as possible. Exposures to the outside air should be limited, extra insulation should be wrapped around pipes, and the addition of protective devices and materials will minimize the possibility of breaks in the plumbing system.

And then the unexpected happens. Let me describe the unexpected woe our family experienced during that first year. Our dishwasher was installed to the right side of our sink, which is a part of a bay window on the front of the home. The sink is the only item within the bay window. In order to connect the dishwasher's water and waste exhaust pipes to the sink/sewer line underneath the sink, the lines had to enter the inside of the wall at the corner where the bay window is attached to the front wall. The hole was successfully drilled during construction and the dishwasher and associated water and waste pipes installed.

In December of 1989, the temperatures plummeted in our Florida city to five degrees above zero, and the pipes in many homes froze solid. We had no problems in our new house except the water and waste lines to the dishwasher. These lines froze for a space of about 6 inches—that 6 inches that came through the wall and exposed the lines inside the wall to the lower temperatures of the outside. Upon investigation, it was discovered that the lines were not adequately insulated against the outside air intrusion into the wall. With a hair dryer set on high/hot, I melted the ice in the frozen lines and stuffed the traverse hole with extra insulation left over from construction, and the problem immediately disappeared, not to return.

Electrical Problems

Electrical problems occur either in the electrical wiring system, the lights/fixtures, or the major appliances. And you can expect the subcontractors or materials suppliers to blame each other when these problems arise.

If a light fixture does not operate properly, you will certainly need to determine whether the problem is in the fixture itself or in the wiring and switch mechanism. This can often be ascertained by turning the switch off and on, by moving the switch from side to side slightly, and by checking light bulbs. There may be times when the problem cannot be specifically identified. In these circumstances, it would probably be best to call the materials supplier and have his service technicians inspect the fixture for damage. If the fixture is found to be operating properly, then call the electrician.

Be careful that the subcontractors and materials suppliers do not get into a "pass the buck" mode. This is why I have stated that it is important to try to determine the problem yourself before calling the service technicians. For example, within three months after we occupied our home, a fluorescent light over the kitchen counter refused to turn on consistently. I called the service department of the supply house from which the fixture was purchased. The service technician came to the house, checked the bulb in the fixture, changed the bulb, declared it repaired, and left. Within hours, the light was still refusing to turn on consistently. The service department was called again. This time, the technician completely changed the light fixture, declared it repaired, and left. And again, within hours, the light was refusing to turn on consistently as it had previously. At this point, I began to play with the switch to the light fixture. Moving the switch from side to side, I could cause the light to blink off and on. At this point, I called the electrician to come and change the switch. He was not too happy about that. After all, he didn't install faulty switches. Nevertheless, he came, and when he arrived, he looked at the light, declared that the problem was in the fixture and was about to leave. I told him to do me a favor and change the switch anyway. He did, and we have had no more difficulty with the light.

This same scenario will also occur with major appliances. Be sure that you remain firm in your stand to get every system operating properly and to your satisfaction during that first year of occupancy. Test your major appliances in every possible way so that you will not incur any expense later for repairs or service. If the problem is the appliance, call the service department of the supplier. If he does not have a service department, he will have a company appointed to provide those repair services. Ask for the name of that company and remind the supplier of the time period you have had the appliance. If the problem is indeed in the electrical system, call the electrician who installed the wiring to perform the repairs.

HVAC Problems

Because the HVAC system is generally so carefully tested and inspected by the building inspectors, you will likely not encounter much difficulty that first year. Numerous tests are conducted on the system to ensure that it works properly, and such tests also offer a sense of security for the homeowner.

With this sense of security, I came home one day to hear a strange noise in the fan of my lower floor HVAC system. When the air conditioner fan was blowing, there was this peculiar sound of air being restricted. The "squirrel cage" type fan also exhibited a variation in sound as it revolved. I tried to analyze the problem but could not figure out the cause of this unusual phenomenon. So I called the HVAC subcontractor. Within a short time, the service technicians came to the house, removed the front cover, and found a piece of cellophane wrapper lodged inside the fan. The wrapper was making the noise and restricting the air as the fan rotated. Nothing more. And the system has worked very well ever since.

This experience does introduce another idea. When your house is under construction, remove as much of the debris as possible from the floors, sills or plates, and walls. Crews tend to eat lunches all through the house, throwing their cans, cigarette butts, candy, and wrappers right where they are. A clean, roughed-in house, even inside the walls, will discourage the attraction of pests and avoid such problems as occurred in the case of our HVAC system.

MINOR PROBLEMS

During the first year of occupancy, you will experience numerous minor difficulties that can easily be repaired either by you or by the subcontractor who was responsible during construction. These minor problems are usually not the cause of major headaches, but they can be annoying. This section provides a list of the kinds of minor troubles you might encounter during that first year.

Pre-wired Elements

Pre-wired elements usually include telephone and TV cable wiring, which are placed inside the walls during construction. Sometimes trouble, requiring attention, can be experienced within these wiring configurations. The sources of assistance in case of telephone wiring trouble would be the local telephone or communications company that serviced the internal jacks and telephone

connections, or the company that installed the telephone wiring in the home, if that company is not a local telephone or communications company. It is always best to obtain maintenance services from the company installing the wiring.

In the case of problems with TV cable, the local cable company or the company installing the wiring, if different, can assist with the trouble. And again, it is best always to enlist the assistance of the installer during this first year of maintenance.

Cracking Concrete

Due to settling and other contributing factors, concrete will tend to crack at points where stress is greatest. In the slab, these cracks will not be noticeable, since you probably will have covered the floor with carpet or some other type of flooring. You may discover such cracks in an area like the garage. Unless the cracks are larger than $1/32$ of an inch wide, no major concern should result. If the cracks are larger than indicated, you may wish to use a patching compound to close the crack to avoid the intrusion of pests, moisture, or other elements that might have an adverse effect upon the interior. As a preventive measure, you may want to include the application of a sealing material on all brick and concrete surfaces used in the home.

Trim Problems

Because of the nature of the trim work, you will likely have little or no trouble with your trim. However, if you discover a cracked piece of trim, whether a floor molding, ceiling molding, chair rail, door frame, or any other trim element, call the subcontractor who installed the trim and have that subcontractor correct the problem.

Sometimes problems occur that are not the fault of the trim installer. For example, during the first six months of our occupancy, we noticed that the panels in all the wood panel doors were separating from the connecting parts, leaving an unstained strip along the outer edge of the panel. Rather than call the door manufacturer, I simply applied stain to the unstained strip with a cotton swab. After drying, I applied a small amount of finishing varnish to the newly stained portion. This corrected the problem.

This problem probably occurred during the time that all the wood doors and trim materials were being pre-stained. In a very hot workshop where the pre-staining work was being performed, the heat of the workshop likely dried out the wood materials, causing the glue inside the grooves eventually to loosen. Since this did not appear to be the fault either of the manufacturer or of the trim installer, I chose to correct the problem myself. The correction procedure was easy and simple.

Air Intrusion

Not until you have occupied the house will you know for sure how well the house will withstand the intrusion of air. I can tell you that I insulated my house so tightly that, with the windows closed, it actually takes two days for the interior of the house to realize that a dramatic change of temperature has occurred outside. Nevertheless, as mentioned above with regard to the dishwasher plumbing, additional insulation was required to prevent the freezing of the pipes to the dishwasher. Also, vents through the walls from the clothes dryer and kitchen exhaust required additional insulation. During the winter, I discovered that the vent pipe from the exhaust fan over the kitchen stove was not insulated sufficiently to keep the air out completely. So the situation simply required that I take a portion of the insulation left over from the construction and insert it around the vent pipe so that the air was cut off completely.

Loose Grout

Every homeowner has experienced having a towel rack fall off the wall or having a piece of tile crack. Well, you can bet that you will have the same experience in your new home. But the solution is quite simple—call the subcontractor. Your tile subcontractor will be glad to come to your home and repair any loosened tiles or loose towel racks or soap dishes. I would not encourage you to take on the responsibility of these kinds of repairs until after the first year.

These are only a few of the minor troubles you might expect during that first year. And it certainly is possible that some of these minor troubles could become major difficulties. If that is the case, be sure to call the appropriate subcontractor to make the repairs. *Do not attempt to make major corrections yourself!* One of the reasons is that your repair job will likely make null and void any maintenance agreement, specified or implied, that may exist not only for the specific problem you addressed but also for the entire system with which the problem is associated.

TROUBLESHOOTING TIPS

When you experience a problem in your new home during that first year, there is a four-step process to help you in deciding what action or actions to take. By using this procedure, you may avoid undue delays in getting the problem corrected.

STEP 1: Determine the specific cause of the problem. To get at the root of the matter and correct the right problem, the specific cause must be ascertained. A good example of this action is that used earlier in this chapter relating to the fluorescent light fixture. What appeared to be a problem with the light fixture actually was trouble with the light switch. Determining that the switch was the problem would have saved us two to three weeks without the use of the light and saved the supplier's service department two trips to our house.

STEP 2: Identify the subcontractor most closely associated with or most likely to be related to the problem.

STEP 3: Identify the extent of the problem. If the problem is minor by nature and you know how to correct it, go ahead and resolve the trouble without involving the subcontractor. However, do not attempt to correct problems of major import since such intrusion may cause your warranty to become null and void.

STEP 4: Once the problem is identified as a major one requiring the hands of experts, prepare to call in those experts. If the problem is in a system installed by a subcontractor, that subcontractor is the one to call for maintenance. If the trouble is determined to be in an ancillary element or component such as a light fixture or major appliance, then call the supplier for service.

IMPLIED WARRANTY

As mentioned in Chapter 7, be sure you have an understanding with each of your subcontractors and your major component suppliers that an implied warranty will exist on all components and labor for a period of one year. This warranty, while not *usually* in writing, is implied with and for every homeowner who purchases a new home. If the home were to be purchased from a licensed contractor, the warranty would be with the contractor. In the case of the self-contractor, the warranty is with the subcontractors and suppliers. For purposes of personal security, you may wish to use the Home Warranty form in the Appendix. Keep that form on file for a period of one year from the date of occupancy. Occupancy will be determined by the date shown on the Certificate of Occupancy.

CONCLUSION

It is now one year after you occupied your new home. You are as proud as ever of the accomplishment of its construction. The problems during the first year have been minimal. You have this home which you can share with your family and friends, a home into which you have poured your very heart and soul. You deserve to relax and enjoy it. But somehow you can't. There is this nagging in your mind that just will not let you go. You just *must* build another house. But then there is that other voice, your spouse saying, "Don't even think about it!" Oh, well, it was a good idea. You probably don't have time anyway.

APPENDIX

PROPERTIES OF INTEREST

Property Location:	
Name of Listing Agent/ Owner (Circle One):	Real Estate Company:
Agent or Owner's Phone No.:	Agent's After Hours Phone No.:
NOTES:	

Property Location:	
Name of Listing Agent/ Owner (Circle One):	Real Estate Company:
Agent or Owner's Phone No.:	Agent's After Hours Phone No.:
NOTES:	

Property Location:	
Name of Listing Agent/ Owner (Circle One):	Real Estate Company:
Agent or Owner's Phone No.:	Agent's After Hours Phone No.:
NOTES:	

COMPARABLE SALES

Location:	
Sales Date:	Sales Price: $
Size:	General Shape:
Conditions of Sale:	
Comments:	

Location:	
Sales Date:	Sales Price: $
Size:	General Shape:
Conditions of Sale:	
Comments:	

Location:	
Sales Date:	Sales Price: $
Size:	General Shape:
Conditions of Sale:	
Comments:	

Location:	
Sales Date:	Sales Price: $
Size:	General Shape:
Conditions of Sale:	
Comments:	

DESIGNER SELECTION SHEET

Instructions: After obtaining the personal information, check the appropriate column which indicates your evaluation of that criterion. Number 1 represents the lowest level while number 5 represents the highest achievement.

Name:	Address:					
Phone No.:	Secretary's Name:					
EVALUATION CRITERIA		1	2	3	4	5
1. Team Player						
2. Available/Accessible						
3. Professional Capability						
4. Practical Approach						
5. Creative/Imaginative						
6. Open-Minded						
7. Clear/Understandable Plans						
Comments:						

Name:	Address:					
Phone No.:	Secretary's Name:					
EVALUATION CRITERIA		1	2	3	4	5
1. Team Player						
2. Available/Accessible						
3. Professional Capability						
4. Practical Approach						
5. Creative/Imaginative						
6. Open-Minded						
7. Clear/Understandable Plans						
Comments:						

CONTRACT WITH DESIGNER

CONTRACT AGREEMENT

THIS AGREEMENT made and entered into by and between _____, hereinafter referred to as "Owner" and _____, hereinafter known as "Designer";

WITNESSETH:

WHEREAS, Designer designs residential construction; and

WHEREAS, Owner has retained Designer to design his personal residence; and

WHEREAS, Owner and Designer desire to put this agreement in writing; and

NOW, THEREFORE, the parties hereto, for and in consideration of the mutual promises herein contained and in the sum of One Dollar ($1.00) and other good and valuable considerations, the receipt whereof is hereby acknowledged, do hereby covenant and agree as follows:

1. Designer agrees to design the personal residence of Owner according to the following phases:

    A. Schematic Design Phase—To provide conceptual scheme, providing the scale and relationship of the project components to meet Owner's requirements; to provide initial estimate of costs.

    B. Design Development Phase — To provide studies applicable for Architectural Review Board consideration; to provide documents which fix and describe the size and character of the project; to provide a revised cost estimate.

    C. Construction Documents Phase—To provide detailed drawings and specifications setting forth the requirements for the construction of all systems within the residence; to provide a final estimate of construction costs.

    D. Bidding/Negotiation Phase—Assist as needed or required.

    E. Construction Phase—To make periodic visits (no less than three times each week) and to be on call for evaluation and recommendation in case of problems or other considerations.

2. Owner agrees to make a fixed fee payment of $ _____ to Designer according to the following schedule:

Retainer	$_____
Completion of Schematic Design Phase	$_____
Completion of Design Development Phase	$_____
Completion of Construction Document Phase	$_____
Completion of Bidding/Negotiation Phase	$_____
Receipt of Certificate of Occupancy	$_____

IN WITNESS WHEREOF, the parties have executed this agreement this _____ day of _____, 19___.

_____   _____
          DESIGNER   OWNER

MS (REG)

OMB No. 2502-0265

A. U.S. DEPARTMENT OF HOUSING AND URBAN DEVELOPMENT	B. TYPE OF LOAN:

B. TYPE OF LOAN:

1. ___ FHA   2. ___ FMHA   3. ___ CONV. UNINS
4. ___ VA   5. ___ CONV. INS

6. FILE NUMBER	7. LOAN NUMBER

8. MORTG. INS. CASE NO.

SETTLEMENT STATEMENT

C. NOTE: This form is furnished to give you a statement of actual settlement costs. Amounts paid to and by the settlement agent are shown. Items marked "(p.o.c.)" were paid outside the closing: they are shown here for informational purposes and are not included in the totals.

D. NAME AND ADDRESS OF BORROWER	E. NAME AND ADDRESS OF SELLER	F. NAME AND ADDRESS OF LENDER

G. PROPERTY LOCATION	H. SETTLEMENT AGENT	I. SETTLEMENT DATE:
	PLACE OF SETTLEMENT	

J. SUMMARY OF BORROWER'S TRANSACTION		K. SUMMARY OF SELLER'S TRANSACTION	
100 GROSS AMOUNT DUE FROM BORROWER:		**400 GROSS AMOUNT DUE TO SELLER:**	
101 Contract sales price		401 Contract sales price	
102 Personal property		402 Personal property	
103 Settlement charges to borrow (*line 1400*)		403	
104		404	
105		405	
Adjustments for items paid by seller in advance:		Adjustments for items paid by seller in advance	
106 City/town taxes to		406 City/town taxes to	
107 County taxes to		407 County taxes to	
108 Assessments to		408 Assessments to	
109		409	
110		410	
111		411	
112		412	
120 GROSS AMOUNT DUE FROM BORROWER:		**420 GROSS AMOUNT DUE TO SELLER:**	
200 AMOUNTS PAID BY OR IN BEHALF OF BORROWER:		**500 REDUCTIONS IN AMOUNT DUE TO SELLER:**	
201 Deposit or earnest money		501 Excess deposit (see instructions)	
202 Principal amount of new loan(s)		502 Settlement charges to seller (*line 1400*)	
203 Existing loan(s) taken subject to		503 Existing loan(s) taken subject to	
204		504 Payoff of first mortgage loan	
205		505 Payoff of second mortgage loan	
206		506	
207		507	
208		508	
209		509	
Adjustments for items unpaid by seller:		Adjustments for items unpaid by seller:	
210 City/town taxes to		510 City/town taxes to	
211 County taxes to		511 County taxes to	
212 Assessments to		512 Assessments to	
213		513	
214		514	
215		515	
216		516	
217		517	
218		518	
219		519	
220 TOTAL PAID BY/FOR BORROWER:		**520 TOTAL REDUCTION AMOUNT DUE TO SELLER:**	
300 CASH AT SETTLEMENT FROM/TO BORROWER:		**600 CASH AT SETTLEMENT TO/FROM BORROWER:**	
301 Gross amount due from borrower (*line 120*)		601 Gross amount due to seller (*line 420*)	
302 Less amounts paid by/for borrower (*line 220*)		602 Less total reductions in amount due seller (*line 520*)	
303 CASH (__FROM) (__TO) BORROWER:		**603 CASH (__TO) (__FROM) SELLER:**	

HUD-1
RESPA, HB 4305.2

03892

SALES ESTIMATE OF MAJOR COMPONENTS

To: _____

Address: _____

Job: *Taylor Residence*

DATE _____ 19 ___

TERMS AND CONDITIONS

TERMS: _____

This estimate is valid for _____ days
After this period prices are subject to change

BY: _____

QTY	DESCRIPTION	UNIT	TOTAL
	— FOOTING —		
51	#5 Rebar (Assuming 2 ea #5 cont all ftgs)	5 23	266 73
24	#4 Rebar (Assuming approx 7' of Bar every 4' of perimeter necessary)	3 15	75 60
100	Rod Chairs	20	20 00
1	Re Tie Wire	2 12	2 12
240 lf	2x4 culls	17	40 80
300 lf	1x4 #2	11	33 00
1	Lg Masons Twine (116 RL)	5 31	5 31
			443 56
	— SLAB —		
4	6x6 Welire Mesh	39 53	158 12
1	32x100 6 mil Poly	85 50	85 50
80	½x6 Bldg Anchor Blts	22	17 60
			261 22
	— 1ST FLOOR FRAME —		
41	2x4x14 PT	3 21	131 61
1	2x6x10 PT	2 96	2 96
640	2x4 LP Studs	1 52	972 80
14	2x6 LP Studs	2 75²	38 53
40	2x4x10 LP	2 05⁵	82 20
75	2x4x12 LP	2 43	182 25
75	2x4x14 LP	2 835	212 63
75	2x4x16 LP	3 28⁸	246 60
8	2x12x10 #2	6 72	53 76
25	2x12x14 #2	11 08⁸	277 20
2	2x12x16 #2	14 46⁴	28 93

Please examine this estimate carefully, as we agree to furnish only the articles named and described in this estimate, regardless of how your inquiry may have read. Clerical errors are subject to correction.

SUB TOTAL	
TAX	
TOTAL	

03896

SALES ESTIMATE OF MAJOR COMPONENTS

To: _____

Address: _____

Job: *Taylor Residence*

DATE _____ 19 ___

TERMS AND CONDITIONS

TERMS: _____

This estimate is valid for _____ days
After this period prices are subject to change

BY: _____

QTY	DESCRIPTION					UNIT	TOTAL
—	Cornice — Assuming Vinal As Vinal Siding is Specified						
1	2×6×20 PT					7 54	7 54
1	2×6×14 PT					4 56	4 54
2	Johnson 1500 Pocket Door Frames					40 46	80 92
2	Rl 14"×50' 3rd Gr Alum Flashing					30 06	60 12
2	Bx Duplex Wall Ties					13 95	27 90
40	2×4×20 LP (Sub Fascia + Blkng)					4 16	166 40
							347 42
	— Roof —						
126	Bx Glassmaster 3TAB 20yr F/G Shingle					6 50	819 80
40	6" Alum Eve Metal DB/BRZ					3 92	156 80
1	Bx 1" Roof Tacks					28 35	28 35
8	Ridge Vent CRV 10 ft.					11 66	93 28
6	RV Connectors					1 31	7 86
4	RV End Plugs					81	3 24
							1108 53
84	— SheetRock —	up 24	dn 50	gar 10	Thru Zenco	6 50	546 00
194	5/8×4×12 Reg	52	128	14		5 15	999 10
	1/2×4×12 Reg						1545 10

Please examine this estimate carefully, as we agree to furnish only the articles named and described in this estimate, regardless of how your inquiry may have read. Clerical errors are subject to correction.

SUB TOTAL	
TAX	
TOTAL	

CUSTOMER COPY

CERTIFICATE OF OCCUPANCY

Building Inspections
CITY OF ANYTOWN BUILDING INSPECTION

Building Permit No.	Date Permit Issued	Date C.O. Issued
89 00005679	06/12/90	09/13/90

Book	SEG1	SEG2	PLATE/BOOK/PAGE
03	5001	020	PBK 02015 PG 0433

ISSUED FOR

SINGLE FAM DWELL DETACHED

OWNER

TAYLOR J. RODNEY
123 OAK DRIVE
ANYTOWN, US 56789

PROPERTY ADDRESS

123 OAK DRIVE

The above was inspected and to the best of my knowledge conforms to all code requirements of the City of Anytown Building Inspection, and is approved for all utility services and
occupancy, for use stated in permit only.

_____

AUTHORIZED SIGNATURE

LOAN INFORMATION GUIDE

Name of Bank: _____ Date: _____

Address of Bank: _____ Nearest Branch: _____

Phone No.: _____ Branch Phone No.: _____

Contact Person: _____

Position: _____

Type of Loan	Availability		Interest Rate	Discount Points	Origination Fee
Construction Loan	Y	N			
Construction-Perm	Y	N			
Conventional Loan	Y	N			
FHA	Y	N			
VA	Y	N			
ARM	Y	N			

_____ Percentage of equity required

_____ Term or maturity of Construction Loan

Permanent Loan Terms available:

___ 15 years ___ 20 years ___ 25 years ___ 30 years

Appraisal required? Y N

Number of "No Fee" draws on construction loan: 1 2 3 4 5 6 7 8 9 10

Amount of Draw Fee: $_____

Insurance required:

Estimated approval time:

Number of required sets of house plans:

2-Year Interest Rate History:

Received Loan Package: Y N

COMMENTS:

BORROWER'S/BUILDER'S ESTIMATE OF COSTS

MATERIALS	QUANTITY	COST
1. Permits, insurance, etc.		
2. Foundation		
(a) Footings		
(b) Piers		
(c) Concrete and reinforcing materials		
(d) Chimney and fireplace materials (brick, mortar, etc.)		
3. Lumber		
(a) Framing		
(b) Sheathing		
(c) Exterior walls and partitions		
(d) Trim and finishing lumber		
(e) Flooring		
(f) Other		
4. Roofing (including felt)		
5. Interior walls and ceiling materials		
6. Millwork		
(a) Doors and door frames		
(b) Windows and window frames		
(c) Screens (doors and windows)		
7. Hardware		
8. Paint		
9. Heating & A/C equip.		
10. Insulation materials		
11. Matls. for sidewalks, driveways, etc.		
12. Nails		
13. Fans		
14. Other items		
15. Sales tax		
TOTAL MATERIALS		

LABOR	
1. Preparation of site: excavation, fill, and landscaping)	
2. Carpentry work	
3. Masonry	
4. Roofing	
5. Painting	
6. Other work	
TOTAL LABOR	

SUB-CONTRACTS	
1. Plumbing	
2. Wiring	
3. Sheet metal work (termite shields, valleys, gutters, etc.)	
4. Grill work	
5. Tile work	
6. Other sub-contracts	
TOTAL SUB-CONTRACTS	

MISCELLANEOUS	

TOTALS	
MATERIALS TOTAL	
LABOR TOTAL	
SUB-CONTRACTS TOTAL	
MISCELLANEOUS TOTAL	

CONSTRUCTION LOAN DISBURSEMENT SCHEDULE

Loan # _____ Owner/Contractor _____

Property Address_____ Legal Description _____

Loan Amount .... $ _____

Less: Closing Costs........................ $ _____

LIP Available for Construction......... $ _____

* Less: Lot Draw .... $ _____

PROCEEDS: * Available for Construction Purposes (LIP Balance)............................. $ _____

* The percentage approved by the inspector will be applied to the balance available for construction purposes to determine the dollar amount to be disbursed after each inspection. NOTE: THERE IS A CHARGE OF $35 FOR EVERY INSPECTION AFTER SIX.

ITEM .... PERCENT	Draws — $35 charge after six							
	(1)	(2)	(3)	(4)	(5)	(6)	(7)	(8)
1. Foundation, subfloor, or slab................12								
2. Rough plumbing 2								
3. Dry in; includes all exterior doors and windows, black board felt and on roof.......................................30								
4. Insulation 2								
5. Roofing 3								
6. Exterior wall finish 8								
7. Interior walls.................................5								
8. Interior trim and doors.....................4								
9. Cabinets......................................3								
10. Fireplace 2								
11. Plumbing, final 3								
12. Ceramic tile or fiberglass tubs 1								
13. Electric rough 2								
14. Electric finish 1								
15. Duct work...................................1								
16. Heater 2								
17. Air conditioner 2								
18. Appliances..................................3								
19. Floor covering 5								
20. Walks & drives.............................3								
21. Landscaping................................2								
22. Painting......................................3								
23. Cleanup 1								

TOTAL PERCENTAGE APPROVED FOR DISBURSEMENT

Disbursements

Authorized by: (initial)	Balance	Received or Deposited by (Signature & Date)
Closing Costs $ _____	$ _____	
_____ Lot _____	$_____	$ _____
_____ #1 _____	$_____	$ _____
_____ #2 _____	$_____	$ _____
_____ #3 _____	$_____	$ _____
_____ #4 _____	$_____	$ _____
_____ #5 _____	$_____	$ _____
_____ #6 _____	$_____	$ _____
_____ #7 _____	$_____	$ _____
_____ #8 _____	$_____	$ _____
TOTAL $ _____	TOTAL SHOULD EQUAL LIP BALANCE (PROCEEDS)	

(1)	(2)	(3)	(4)	(5)	(6)	(7)	(8)

Inspectors should sign and date on lines above

Comments:

MORTGAGE CHECKLIST

Instructions: Have your bank contact person complete this checklist.

Name of Bank:_____

Address of Bank:_____ Nearest Branch: _____

Bank Phone No.:_____ Branch Phone No.:_____

Contact Person: _____

Position: _____

MORTGAGE AMOUNT: $_____

Basic Features

Fixed rate annual percentage rate:	_____	20 years
(This is the cost of your credit as a yearly rate	_____	25 years
which includes interest and other charges.)	_____	30 years

ARM annual percentage rate
    Adjustment period   _____
    Index used and current rate   _____
    Margin   _____
    Initial payment without discount   _____
    Initial payment with discount   _____
    How long will discount last?   _____
    Interest rate caps: periodic   _____
                            overall   _____
    Payment caps   _____
    Negative amortization   _____
    Convertibility or prepayment privilege   _____
    Initial fees and charges   _____

Monthly Payment Amounts

What will my monthly payment be after 12 months if the index rate:
    stays the same?   _____
    goes up 2%   _____
    goes down 2%   _____
What will my monthly payment be after 3 years if the index rate:
    stays the same?   _____
    goes up 2% per year   _____
    goes down 2% per year   _____

SAMPLE FNMA FORM 1003

Residential Loan Application

[1] MORTGAGE APPLIED FOR: ☒ Conventional ☐ FHA ☐ VA ☐ — | Amount $86,000. | Interest Rate 10.5% | No. of Months 360 | Monthly Payment Principal & Interest $ | Escrow/Impounds (to be collected monthly) ☐ Taxes ☐ Hazard Ins. ☐ Mtg. Ins. ☐ _____

Prepayment Option

[2] **Subject Property**

Property Street Address: 1402 Berkley Road | City: Montgomery | County: Montgomery | State: AL | Zip: 36111 | No. Units: 1

Legal Description (Attach description if necessary): Lot 4, Block E, Normandale, Plat Book 20, page 22 | Year Built: 1960

Purpose of Loan: ☒ Purchase ☐ Construction-Permanent ☐ Construction ☐ Refinance ☐ Other (Explain)

Complete this line if Construction-Permanent or Construction Loan: Lot Value Data | Year Acquired | Original Cost $ | Present Value (a) $ | Cost of Imps. (b) $ | Total (a + b) $ | ENTER TOTAL AS PURCHASE PRICE IN DETAILS OF PURCHASE.

Complete this line if a Refinance Loan: Year Acquired $ | Original Cost $ | Amt. Existing Liens $ | Purpose of Refinance | Describe Improvements [ ] made [ ] to be made | Cost: $

Title Will Be Held In What Name(s): John J. and Karen W. Brown | Manner In Which Title Will Be Held

Source of Down Payment and Settlement Charges: Personal funds

[3] This application is designed to be completed by the borrower(s) with the lender's assistance. The Co-Borrower Section and all other Co-Borrower questions must be completed and the appropriate box(es) checked if ☒ another person will be jointly obligated with the Borrower on the loan, or ☐ the Borrower is relying on income from alimony, child support or separate maintenance or on the income or assets of another person as a basis for repayment of the loan, or ☐ the Borrower is married and resides, or the property is located, in a community property state.

[4]

	Borrower	Co-Borrower
Name	John J. Brown — Age 9-3-51 — School Yrs 18	Karen W. Brown — Age 4-20-55 — School Yrs 12
Present Address	No. Years 5 ☐ Own ☒ Rent	No. Years 5 ☐ Own ☒ Rent
Street	4401 Madras Lane Apt. 402	Same
City/State/Zip	Montgomery, AL 36108	Same
Former address if less than 2 years at present address		
Street		
City/State/Zip		
Years at former address	☐ Own ☐ Rent	☐ Own ☐ Rent
Marital Status	☒ Married ☐ Separated ☐ Unmarried (incl. single, divorced, widowed) — DEPENDENTS 2 — AGES 4,10	☒ Married ☐ Separated ☐ Unmarried (incl. single, divorced, widowed)
Name and Address of Employer	Acme Engineering, 402 Decatur Street, Montgomery, AL 36104	Gayfers, 3000 Eastdale Mall, Montgomery, AL 36117
Years employed in this line of work or profession?	9 years — Years on this job 1 ☐ Self Employed	8 years — Years on this job 8 ☐ Self Employed
Position/Title	Project Manager	Sales Clerk
Type of Business	Const. Engineering	Retail
Social Security Number	410-24-4586	423-43-1523
Home Phone	205/288-8888	205/288-8888
Business Phone	205/834-2222	205/282-4444

[5] **[6]** **[7]**

Gross Monthly Income					Monthly Housing Expense**			Details of Purchase	
Item	Borrower	Co-Borrower	Total	Rent	$585.	PRESENT	PROPOSED	Do Not Complete If Refinance	
Base Empl. Income	$3500.	$850.	$4350.	First Mortgage (P&I)		$		a. Purchase Price	$
Overtime				Other Financing (P&I)				b. Total Closing Costs (Est.)	
Bonuses				Hazard Insurance				c. Prepaid Escrows (Est.)	
Commissions				Real Estate Taxes				d. Total (a + b + c)	$
Dividends/Interest				Mortgage Insurance				e. Amount This Mortgage	( )
Net Rental Income				Homeowner Assn. Dues				f. Other Financing	( )
Other† (before completing, see notice under Describe Other Income below.)				Other				g. Other Equity	( )
				Total Monthly Pmt.	$525.	$		h. Amount of Cash Deposit	( )
				Utilities	75.			i. Closing Costs Paid by Seller	( )
Total	$3500.	$850.	$4350.	Total	$600.	$		j. Cash Reqd. For Closing (Est.)	$

[8] **Describe Other Income**

◇ B—Borrower C—Co-Borrower | NOTICE: † Alimony, child support, or separate maintenance income need not be revealed if the Borrower or Co-Borrower does not choose to have it considered as a basis for repaying this loan. | Monthly Amount $

[9] **If Employed In Current Position For Less Than Two Years, Complete the Following**

B/C	Previous Employer/School	City/State	Type of Business	Position/Title	Dates From/To	Monthly Income
B	Blank Bros. Engineering	Montgomery, AL	Const. Engineering	Proj. Mgr.	1/82-6/86	$2,250.

[10] **These Questions Apply To Both Borrower and Co-Borrower**

If a "yes" answer is given to a question in this column, please explain on an attached sheet.

	Borrower Yes or No	Co-Borrower Yes or No
Are there any outstanding judgments against you?	no	no
Have you been declared bankrupt within the past 7 years?	no	no
Have you had property foreclosed upon or given title or deed in lieu thereof in the last 7 years?	no	no
Are you a party to a law suit?	no	no
Are you obligated to pay alimony, child support, or separate maintenance?	no	no
Is any part of the down payment borrowed?	no	no
Are you a co-maker or endorser on a note?	no	no

	Borrower Yes or No	Co-Borrower Yes or No
Are you a U.S. citizen?	yes	yes
If "no," are you a resident alien?		
If "no," are you a non-resident alien?		

Explain Other Financing or Other Equity (if any). _____

*FHLMC FNMA require business credit report, signed Federal Income Tax returns for last two years; and, if available, audited Profit and Loss Statement plus balance sheet for same period.

**All Present Monthly Housing Expenses of Borrower and Co-Borrower should be listed on a combined basis.

***Optional for FHLMC

FHLMC 65 Rev. 10/86

L-130 A.

Fannie Mae Form 1003 Rev. 10/86

[11] This Statement and any applicable supporting schedules may be completed jointly by both married and unmarried co-borrowers if their assets and liabilities are sufficiently joined so that the Statement can be meaningfully and fairly presented on a combined basis; otherwise separate Statements and Schedules are required (FHLMC 65A/FNMA 1003A). If the co-borrower section was completed about a spouse, this statement and supporting schedules must be completed about that spouse also. ☒ Completed Jointly ☐ Not Completed Jointly

[12]

Assets		Liabilities and Pledged Assets				

Indicate by (*) those liabilities or pledged assets which will be satisfied upon sale of real estate owned or upon refinancing of subject property.

Description	Cash or Market Value	Creditors' Name, Address and Account Number		Acct. Name if Not Borrower's	Mo. Pmt. and Mos. Left to Pay	Unpaid Balance
[13] Cash Deposit Toward Purchase Held By Bond Realty	1000.	Installment Debts (Include "revolving" charge accounts) Co. AmSouth VISA Addr. P.O. Box 451 City Montgomery, AL	Acct. No. 461-348-533	Pmt/Mos	25.1	250.
Institutions (Account Numbers) Bank, S & L or Credit Union AmSouth Bank Addr. P.O. Box 431 City Montgomery, AL Acct. No. 4235487	5,425.	Co. Gayfers Addr. City	Acct. No. 145-876-54325		-0-	-0-
Bank, S & L or Credit Union Merrill Lynch Addr. P.O. Box 2111 City Montgomery Acct. No. 3611254	2,000.	Co. Addr. City	Acct. No.		/	
Bank, S & L or Credit Union Addr. City Acct. No.		Co. Addr. City Other Debts including Stock Pledges	Acct. No.		/	
Stocks and Bonds (No./Description)		Real Estate Loans Co.	Acct. No.		/	
200 Shrs. B&Q Prod.	840.	Addr. City			╳	
Life Insurance Net Cash Value Face Amount $ 250,000.	-0-	Co. Addr. City				
Subtotal Liquid Assets	9,265.					
Real Estate Owned (Enter Market Value from Schedule of Real Estate Owned)		Automobile Loans Co. GMAC Addr. 100 East Drive City Bhm AL	Acct. No. 52356		188.124	4500.
Vested Interest in Retirement Fund	5,800.	Co.	Acct. No.		/	
Net worth of Business Owned (ATTACH FINANCIAL STATEMENT)		Co. City			/	
Automobiles Owned (Make and Year) 84 Chevrolet Caprice	2500.					
86 Buick Century	7000.					
Furniture and Personal Property	10,000.	Alimony/Child Support/Separate Maintenance Payments Owed to			/	╳
Other Assets (Itemize) Honda Motorcylee	1,000.	Total Monthly Payments			213.	
Total Assets	35,565	Net Worth (A minus B) 30,815.			Total Liabilities	4750.

SCHEDULE OF REAL ESTATE OWNED (If Additional Properties Owned Attach Separate Schedule)							
Address of Property (Indicate S if Sold, PS if Pending Sale or R if Rental being held for income)	Type of Property	Present Market Value	Amount of Mortgages & Liens	Gross Rental Income	Mortgage Payments	Taxes, Ins. Maintenance and Misc.	Net Rental Income
		$	$	$	$	$	$
[14] TOTALS →		$	$	$	$	$	$

List Previous Credit References

B-Borrower C-Co-Borrower	Creditor's Name and Address	Account Number	Purpose	Highest Balance	Date Paid
				$	

List any additional names under which credit has previously been received _____

[15] AGREEMENT: The undersigned applies for the loan indicated in this application to be secured by a first mortgage or deed of trust on the property described herein, and represents that the property will not be used for any illegal or restricted purpose, and that all statements made in this application are true and are made for the purpose of obtaining the loan. Verification may be obtained from any source named in this application. The original or a copy of this application will be retained by the lender, even if the loan is not granted. The undersigned ☒ intend or ☐ do not intend to occupy the property as their primary residence.

I/we fully understand that it is a federal crime punishable by fine or imprisonment, or both, to knowingly make any false statements concerning any of the above facts as applicable under the provisions of Title 18, United States Code, Section 1014.

[16] *John T. Brown* Borrower's Signature Date 6/5/88   *Karen W. Brown* Co-Borrower's Signature Date 6/5/88

[17] **Information for Government Monitoring Purposes**

The following information is requested by the Federal Government for certain types of loans related to a dwelling, in order to monitor the lender's compliance with equal credit opportunity and fair housing laws. You are not required to furnish this information, but are encouraged to do so. The law provides that a lender may neither discriminate on the basis of this information, nor on whether you choose to furnish it. However, if you choose not to furnish it, under Federal regulations this lender is required to note race and sex on the basis of visual observation or surname. If you do not wish to furnish the above information, please check the box below. (Lender must review the above material to assure that the disclosures satisfy all requirements to which the Lender is subject under applicable state law for the particular type of loan applied for.)

Borrower: ☐ I do not wish to furnish this information   Co-Borrower: ☐ I do not wish to furnish this information
Race/National Origin | Race/National Origin
[ ] American Indian, Alaskan Native ☒ Asian, Pacific Islander   [ ] American Indian, Alaskan Native [ ] Asian, Pacific Islander
[ ] Black [ ] Hispanic ☒ White   [ ] Black [ ] Hispanic ☒ White
[ ] Other (specify)   [ ] Other (specify)
Sex: [ ] Female ☒ Male   Sex: ☒ Female [ ] Male

[18] **To Be Completed by Interviewer**

This application was taken by:
☐ face to face interview
☐ by mail
☐ by telephone

_____ Interviewer

_____ Name of Interviewer's Employer

_____ Interviewer's Phone Number

_____ Address of Interviewer's Employer

FHLMC Form 65 Rev. 10/88   REVERSE   Fannie Mae Form 1003 Rev. 10/86

HOME LOAN APPLICATION CHECKLIST

In any application process, certain kinds of information are required to be on file with the lender. The following is a checklist of these items. Since policies differ among lenders, other information not listed here may be required. You are advised to check with the lenders to determine the specific data demanded.

1 Residence/ Employment

____ Complete address for 2 years preceding application. Names and addresses of landlords.

____ All employment for 2 years preceding application. Name of company, address, and person to contact.

____ Social Security number(s)

2 List of Assets

____ Checking account numbers and balances

____ Savings account numbers and balances

____ Names and certificate numbers of stocks and bonds

____ Face and cash value of life insurance policies

____ Location and amount of retirement funds

____ Year, model, and estimated value of automobiles

____ Real estate - Type property, value, amount of liens, payment amounts. If you plan to sell this property to buy a new home, you need a copy of the closing statement prior to closing on the new home. If it's rental property, you need a rent or lease agreement.

3 Self-Employed or Working on a Commission Basis

____ 2 years tax returns

____ 2 years profit & loss statements

____ 2 years W-2's

____ Current balance sheet

4 List of Liabilities

Any debts you are presently obligated to pay; company name, address, account number, balance

____ Installments

____ Short-term liabilities

____ Revolving charge accounts

____ Auto loans

____ Real estate loans

____ Alimony or child support

If you are obligated to pay alimony or child support, you need a copy of the divorce decree. If you receive alimony or child support and you plan to state it as income, you need a copy of the divorce decree and proof of receipt.

5 Veteran Seeking a V.A. Loan

____ DD-214 (Separation Record) or Certificate of Eligibility, or a statement from your commanding officer if you are on active duty

6 Your Application Appointment

Bring to the appointment:

____ Contract to purchase home

____ Credit report deposit

____ Appraisal deposit

7 Bankruptcy Ever Declared

____ Copy of the petition and discharge

____ Personal, handwritten explanation of the reason for the action

SETTLEMENT COST WORKSHEET

Name of Bank: _____ Date: _____

Phone No.: _____ Contact Person: _____

800. ITEMS PAYABLE IN CONNECTION WITH LOAN: _____ _____

801. Loan origination fee	%	_____
802. Loan discount	%	_____
803. Appraisal fee	to	_____
804. Credit report	to	_____
805. Lender's inspection fee		_____
806. Mortgage insurance application fee	to	_____
807. Assumption fee		_____
808.		_____
809.		_____
810.		_____
811.		_____

900. ITEMS REQUIRED BY LENDER TO BE PAID IN ADVANCE: _____

901. Interest from	to	@$	per day _____
902. Mortgage insurance premium for		months to	_____
903. Hazard insurance premium for		years to	_____
904.		years to	_____
905.			_____

1000. RESERVES DEPOSITED WITH LENDER: _____

1001. Hazard insurance	months @$	per month	_____
1002. Mortgage insurance	months @$	per month	_____
1003. City property taxes	months @$	per month	_____
1004. County property taxes	months @$	per month	_____
1005. Annual assessments	months @$	per month	_____
1006.	months @$	per month	_____
1007.	months @$	per month	_____
1008.	months @$	per month	_____

1100. TITLE CHARGES: _____

1101. Settlement or closing fee	to	_____
1102. Abstract or title search	to	_____
1103. Title examination	to	_____
1104. Title insurance binder	to	_____
1105. Document preparation	to	_____
1106. Notary fees	to	_____
1107. Attorney's fees	to	_____
(includes above item numbers)		_____
1108. Title insurance	to	_____
(includes above item numbers)		_____
1109. Lender's coverage	$	_____
1110. Owner's coverage	$	_____
1111.		_____
1112.		_____
1113.		_____

1200. GOVERNMENT RECORDING AND TRANSFER CHARGES: _____

1201. Recording fees: Deed $	Mortgage $	Release $	_____
1202. City/county tax/stamps: Deed $		Mortgage $	_____
1203. State tax/stamps: Deed $		Mortgage $	_____
1204.			_____
1205.			_____

1300. ADDITIONAL SETTLEMENT CHARGES: _____

1301. Survey	to	_____
1302. Pest inspection	to	_____
1303.		_____
1304.		_____
1305.		_____

1400. TOTAL SETTLEMENT CHARGES:

_____ _____

SATISFACTORY COMPLETION CERTIFICATE

On _____, 19_____, the property situated at

_____

_____

_____

was appraised by me or _____ .

The appraisal report was subject to: _____ satisfactory completion, _____ repairs, or

_____ .

I certify that I have reinspected subject property, the requirements or conditions set forth in the appraisal report have been met and any required repairs or completion items have been done in a workmanlike manner.

Itemized below are substantial changes from the data in the appraisal report, and these changes do not adversely affect any property ratings or final estimate of value in the report:

_____   _____
DATE   INSPECTOR

SAMPLE BUILDING PERMIT

MECHANICAL INSPECTIONS

CITY OF

INSPECTION DIVISION

ROUGH INSP. _____ BY _____ DATE _____

FINAL INSP. _____ BY _____ DATE _____

GAS TEST _____ BY _____ DATE _____

NOTICE:
In addition to the requirements of this permit, there may be additional restrictions applicable to this property that may be found in the public records of this county.

BUILDING PERMIT

No.

_____

Street Address _____

Date Issued _____ **By** _____

BUILDING INSPECTIONS

Footing Insp. _____ By _____ Date _____

Slab Insp. _____ By _____ Date _____

Framing Insp. _____ By _____ Date _____

Other Insp. _____ By _____ Date _____

Final Insp. _____ By _____ Date _____

GAS INSPECTIONS

Rough Insp. _____ By _____ Date _____

Final Insp. _____ By _____ Date _____

ELECTRICAL INSPECTIONS

Rough Insp. _____ By _____ Date _____

Final Insp. _____ By _____ Date _____

PLUMBING INSPECTIONS

Rough Insp. _____ By _____ Date _____

Stackout Insp. _____ By _____ Date _____

Sewer Insp. _____ By _____ Date _____

Final Insp. _____ By _____ Date _____

"FAILURE TO COMPLY WITH THE MECHANIC'S LIEN LAW CAN RESULT IN THE PROPERTY OWNER PAYING TWICE FOR BUILDING IMPROVEMENTS."

BUILDING MATERIALS SUPPLIERS

Construction Component:		Name of Supplier:	
Address of Supplier:			
Telephone No.:		Contact Person:	

REFERENCE DATE	MATERIALS DESCRIPTION	UNIT PRICE

This price list is good for _____ days from the reference date.

_____
Authorized Signature

GENERAL SUPPLIERS

Name of Supplier: _____ Date: _____

Address of Supplier: _____ Phone No.: _____

Contact Person: _____ These prices are valid for _____ days.

	Unit Price			Unit Price
Footings/Foundation			**Roofing**	
Rebar			Felt	
Rod chairs			Shingles	
Tie wires			Roofing nails	
1 x 4 #2			Flashing	
Slab			Eave metal	
Wire mesh			**Drywall**	
6 mil poly			5/8 x 4 x 12	
Anchor bolts			1/2 x 4 x 12	
Framing			Tape	
2 x 4 x 14			Compound	
2 x 6 x 10			**Trim**	
2 x 4 LP studs			Shoe mold	
2 x 6 LP			Crown mold	
2 x 4 x 10 LP			Chair rail	
2 x 4 x 12 LP			Window sills	
2 x 4 x 14 LP			Exterior vinyl	
2 x 12 x 10 #2			**Miscellaneous**	
2 x 12 x 14 #2			Paint	
2 x 12 x 16 #2			Wallpaper	
2 x 6 x 14 LP			Insulation	
2 x 6 x 14 #2			Fireplace	
2 x 8 x 10 #2				
#10 nails				
#12 nails				
#16 nails				
Rafter ties				
3/4" oxboard				
Decking/Sheathing				
1/2" oxboard				
1/2" plywood				
Plywood clips				
Square cap nails				
Styrofoam				
Soundboard				
Thermoply				

Exterior doors -- use a separate schedule. Interior doors -- use a separate schedule.

_____
Authorized Signature

SUPPLIERS TO BE USED

Company Name: _____

Address: _____

Phone No.: _____ Contact Person: _____

Terms of Payment: _____

Prices good for _____ days from _____.
                                    (date)

Materials Description	Unit Price

Notes:

PROSPECTIVE SUBCONTRACTORS

Subcontractor Specialty:	Company Name:

Owner's Name:
(If different from company name)

Subcontractor Phone No:	Source of Prospect:

NOTES:

Subcontractor Specialty:	Company Name:

Owner's Name:
(If different from company name)

Subcontractor Phone No:	Source of Prospect:

NOTES:

Subcontractor Specialty:	Company Name:

Owner's Name:
(If different from company name)

Subcontractor Phone No:	Source of Prospect:

NOTES:

PROJECT SUBCONTRACTORS

Subcontractor Specialty	Company Name/Owner Name or Contact Person	Phone No.	Job Price

GENERAL LEDGER

DATE	EXPENDITURE (VENDOR)	CK#	DEBITS		CREDITS		BALANCE	

BALANCE

WAIVER OF LIEN FORM

We, the undersigned, as general contractors, subcontractors, materialmen, or others furnishing services, labor, or materials, in the construction or repair of improvements upon real estate owned by:

_____

_____

_____

described as follows:

_____

_____

_____

_____

In consideration of $1.00 to each of us in hand, paid receipt whereof is hereby acknowledged, and other benefits accruing to us, and in order to procure the making of one or more loans on said real estate, as improved, we do hereby waive, release, and quitclaim in favor of the said proposed lender, all right that we may now or hereafter have to a lien upon the land and improvements above described, by virtue of the laws of the State of _____ ; and we do further warrant that we have not assigned our claim for payment nor our right to perfect a lien against said property, and that we have the right to execute this waiver and release thereof.

We further warrant that the contract price to us for the erection of improvements on said property has been paid in full and that all subcontractors and/or all laborers employed in the construction of said premises have been fully paid, and that none of said subcontractors and/or laborers has any claim or lien against said premises.

WITNESS OUR HAND SEAL THIS THE _____ DAY OF _____, 19___ .

_____

_____

CONSTRUCTION MANAGER LOCATOR

Prospective Manager's Name:		Interested
		Not Interested

Phone No:	Source of Prospect:

REFERENCE ADDRESSES	NOTES

SUPPLY HOUSE COMMENTS:

Prospective Manager's Name:		Interested
		Not Interested

Phone No:	Source of Prospect:

REFERENCE ADDRESSES	NOTES

SUPPLY HOUSE COMMENTS:

CONSTRUCTION MANAGEMENT CONTRACT

THIS AGREEMENT made and entered into by and between _____, hereinafter referred to as "Owner" and _____, hereinafter referred to as "Manager";

WITNESSETH:

WHEREAS, Manager constructs residences and manages residential construction; and

WHEREAS, Owner has retained Manager to manage construction of his/her personal residence; and

WHEREAS, Owner and Manager desire to put this agreement in writing; and

NOW, THEREFORE, the parties hereto, for and in consideration of the mutual promises herein contained and in the sum of One Dollar ($1.00) and other good and valuable considerations, the receipt whereof is hereby acknowledged, do hereby covenant and agree as follows:

1. Manager agrees to administer, manage, and supervise the construction of the personal residence of Owner, duties which include:

   A. Setting up of temporary power pole.
   B. Supervising and managing all subcontractors obtained by Owner.
   C. Seeing that all subcontractors are on the job, on time.
   D. Calling for and being present for all inspections by regulatory agencies.
   E. Ordering materials for the job site from vendors selected by Owner.
   F. Other such duties as Owner may deem material to the supervisory function.
   G. Securing bids on such work as called for by Owner.

2. Owner agrees to provide support to Manager as deemed necessary and will be responsible for:

   A. Providing Manager with names of and contract agreements with each subcontractor.
   B. Paying all subcontractors as agreed upon with that subcontractor.
   C. Paying all materials invoices on time as required by vendor.
   D. Paying Manager according to the following schedule:

   (1) $ _____ foundation and slab in place
   (2) $ _____ dry in and rough-ins complete
   (3) $ _____ interior/exterior wall finish complete
   (4) $ _____ trim-outs complete, painting/wallpaper complete, ready for finished flooring
   (5) $ _____ upon completion and receipt of all applicable inspections

IN WITNESS WHEREOF, the parties have executed this agreement this _____ day of _____, 19___.

_____   _____
MANAGER   OWNER

AMENITIES PRICING

AMENITY	SUPPLIER	MATERIALS COSTS	LABOR COSTS

HOME WARRANTY FORM

I (WE), THE UNDERSIGNED, do hereby guarantee and warranty our products or services for a period of one year from the date shown on the Certificate of Occupancy to be issued by _____ [City/County] in compliance with local statutes. If, during such period of normal use, the product or service becomes or indicates defects in materials or workmanship, I (We) will warranty the product or service by correcting the problem(s) without charge.

This warranty is issued solely for the products or services included at _____ [Address] and for the benefit of _____ [Name of Self-Contractor]. This warranty is limited to the original contractor/homeowner and is not transferable. The warranty does not cover damage due to accidents, abuse, tampering, or misuse, nor does it cover damage resulting from service by a person or persons other than the company or person named herein.

_____
COMPANY NAME

_____
AUTHORIZED SIGNATURE

_____
DATE

INDEX